TESTIMONIALS

"India can take you on a deep dive within to come out on the other side, into the beauty of who you really are."

~ Suzanne Stebila ~ *Shaman, Friend, Mentor & Abundant Maker*

*

"India has an incredible ability to bring your shadow forward—quickly. To go as deep and as dark as India has in her journey and to come out the other side—whole—is her Superpower! She has no fear; she can dive as deep and dark as it takes to support you. She's been there. She's been in your shoes and knows exactly where you are in your life, in your process, or in your worst hell. "She holds incredible confidence, in her work, and I have witnessed this in her for many years. You will always feel SAFE with India—no doubt!"

~ Angela Howard ~ *Founder "WildHeart Expressive"*

*

BURNING DOWN THE HOUSE

Transforming Yourself
Into a Powerful New Life

INDIA ZOE PREMA

ISBN: 979-8-9877585-1-9 (Paperback)
ISBN: 979-8-9877585-2-6 (Ebook)

Stephen Henderson
TheArtofBeautyPhotography.com
Metamorphosis Photographic Studio Sedona AZ

Published by Warrior Spirit

*My house
is out of the ordinary.
That's right, don't want to hurt nobody.
Some things sure can—sweep me off my feet.
Burning down the house.*

–David Byrne/Talking Heads

*

Life's a bitch. You've got to go out and kick ass.

–Maya Angelou

*

Set your life on fire, seek those who fan your flames.

–Rumi

YOUR GUIDE TO WHAT'S INSIDE

INTRODUCTION
HERE WE GO

BURNING DOWN THE HOUSE is as transparent and real as I can make it. I hope you enjoy that approach. It's the only way I know how to be.

A created life requires courage and curiosity. We face fear and dig deep and return to the loving essence of who we are—with more grit, grace, and backbone. It's not easy. It isn't meant to be. That's why there is more *ordinary* in the world than *extraordinary*. Reaching for extraordinary is hard. But it's also a blast. Out of the comfort zone is uncomfortable by design, but it's also a hell of an adventure. It takes something big and wild and trusting to go after a big transformation-time and again. It's a big-damned deal for a reason. It takes guts, guts we never knew we had until the situation presents itself.

I've experienced transformation so deep I've set my life on fire several times, come back from nothing again and again, and redefined myself by rising from the ashes newly born. And I've had lots of amazing help show up in my life—a few old friends and many new ones, the teachers who were there when the student was ready, and the friends who are also up to big transformational work. We did it as a team, supporting each other on our individual journeys.

1

We are a species wired for connection. Hopefully, this book will send you into the arms of your beloved, your family, and your circle of friends. It can point you toward a new guide, healer, mentor, sherpa, or shaman. It can inspire you to listen to the deep inner wisdom you have access to as soon as you *come into* self-awareness and have some training in how to access it.

We thrive when we have healthy communities of support. Who you choose to share your bed with, surround your life with, and collaborate with creates the environment that nurtures your growth and evolution. Choosing poorly out of fear, lack of self-love, unhealed stuff, or lack of self-awareness can really turn your life upside down. Choosing wisely offers greater insight, ease, and freedom.

Our best shot at breaking through challenges and loneliness is to learn from each other—but as equals, peer-to-peer. The age of the guru is over and done. The unhealthy dynamic of people claiming special authority, unique power, and super-secret access to knowledge, a connection to Source—that only they claim to possess—is arrogant and manipulative.

I've been in the trenches, and I'm great at supporting people in their expansion and evolution through discovering their shadow, and I attend to my growth all the time as well. I observe, learn, and course correct. I support people who feel the pull to work with me for my kind of transformation. While I still fall short in some areas, my commitment is to always learn and grow, to go inward, and not become enamored by anyone. It's time we all grow the fuck up and become self-responsible rather than be followers who turn our power and venerate another person with higher authority.

Everyone has their unique ways of being gifted, and those differences are to be honored and celebrated, as no one should ever claim a divine right to control another. The guru/devotee dynamic of the past created all sorts of misconduct and slowed everyone's growth. We're seeing the shift globally now, and it's a deep one. Power corrupts and creates dependence. That's why I say the age of the guru is done—stick-a-fork-in-it done.

I believe sharing transparently, honestly, and vulnerably is one key to finding our way forward. Telling the truth to ourselves and each other, finding the humor in the ungraceful, the ugly, or the embarrassing truth. In our authenticity, we lean on and learn from each other and, most importantly, remain sovereign throughout the process of our transformation.

It's harder to take responsibility for our lives than it is to turn our (inner)authority over to others. It's more challenging to admit - how we respond to circumstances creates our experience. We can do hard things. Hard things can be magical, mystical, and transformative if we allow for it. I've learned from many teachers on my path, those who triggered me repeatedly, who offered me the opportunity to course correct my emotions and my energy. I, in turn, give back by leading and guiding others in what I've learned. It's important to share my experience, strength, and hope. I don't overstep my bounds and pretend to know things beyond what I've experienced—just know that it's been a deep, deep well of discovery. I always continue to learn from others who walk their talk, who see their shadow or blind spots and work within them. I'm open to learning continually from Spirit, Source, my Higher Self, and updating things constantly because today's transformation is what we line the birdcage with tomorrow. The ego is sneaky and gets up to all sorts of fuckery! But the soul is persistent and wise. Authenticity and transparency keep us learning and sharing with integrity, and together, we lift each other up.

I hope you are inspired to seek and find your empowering tribe for every step of the journey, including this one. Is there someone you know who can read this book at the same time as you, so you can work on it together? Is your family open to reading and sharing, or a group of close friends of *yours?* It could be more fun for you to share the ride. And please know that the teachers, books, workshops, friends, and experiences that you are drawn to, are likely to change over time as you grow. That's the nature of transformation.

Remember when you were a kid, and as your body grew, you got clothes the next size bigger and handed the clothes you had outgrown to someone who was just the right size for them? It's like that. There is no hierarchy or judgement about where you are or where someone else is. We're all growing alongside each other, and we all need the clothes that fit—at the time.

My tribe—I love them. They are the ones who get it done, the ones who balls-out go for it. And who do I serve? The people who are naturally curious and open. The ones who feel butterflies in their belly and decide that's the sign *it's go time*—even though it scares the shit out of them. I'm a fucking spiritual warrior badass, not because I know more or am better than or was even graceful for any of my badass-ism! Quite the contrary. It takes courage—fucking courage—to go inward and deep into the parts of us we don't, or can't, look at or even see. I was so ungraceful—flailing around like an absolute fish out of water for many years. I didn't know what I didn't know but thought I knew it all. Can you relate?

I also attract those who understand it's possible to learn from each other without having to sink as low as I did in order to "get it."

For instance, because I face planted in a plate of cocaine and drank myself to my moral bottom by the age of 25, you can learn from my breakdown and perhaps skip that option, choosing instead a path of personal growth that includes staying healthy and sober, if need be - all the way through. Do you need to lose your self-respect, any self-love you may have garnered, and all your money to learn? I did, but perhaps you'll get it through osmosis and not have to go there yourself.

In this book, we'll keep our sense of humor while looking at some hard stuff. I hope you find this reading inspiring, thought provoking, and hopeful, with playfulness sprinkled throughout. A human being—BEing Human—can be intriguing, fascinating, indignant, a bunch of things really, and we can also be entertaining and hilarious. When we understand that we are *energetic Beings* in a meat suit, having a physical experience, on a dense planet twirling in a massive galaxy, we can start to see the ridiculousness of the human condition and laughing at ourselves help us navigate the darkness and the day-to-day mundane. Is your spirit free and alive in the mundane?

My experience laid out in this book neither diagnoses nor treats, nor is it a substitute for therapeutic support that can only be provided by those qualified to deal with mental illness, personality disorders, and trauma. This is a book for people in a position to safely take on the exploration of their lives and personal transformation.

This is my story, and to the extent you want it to be, it can be a way of delving into your story as well. Like old friends enjoying a long lunch in the sun or cuddling up warming ourselves at the campfire, we can have a nice chat. In these pages, I'll share my life and invite you to do the same.

We're going to get down and dirty. I encourage you to write in the pages of this book. I'd prefer that you mess this book up; read it in a coffee shop and start a conversation with a friend or stranger, spill food on the book, turn down the corners to mark your place, write in the margins, get it wet in the bathtub, and rip out pages and stick them on your bathroom mirror. There's no need to keep this book pristine. This is not about lofty ideas and book learning; it's about actual lived experiences, and experience is as messy as a bunch of kindergarten kids painting with pudding.

If you want to let the past go, really go, after you're done with this book and have integrated new ways of being, you could burn it. Burn it along with the stuff you don't need hanging around, perhaps old love notes from a relationship that ended, so you can finally release that person with love and gratitude and not have your new love find them in a drawer and wonder why you kept them. You could burn this book with that extra copy of a court document or photo that is part of what ties you to a past way of being and causes you unnecessary suffering.

Once you processed things and reached the forgiveness of others, or found the gratitude for them, and self-forgiveness, put it down, let it go, surrender. You can burn this book with the intention of letting emotions, reminiscing, and storytelling go. Burn it and dance in the light of the flames.

I express anger 41 times throughout. I use the word "fuck," a whopping 73 times. "Fuck," is my power word. It's best you know that upfront. As I wrote this book, the word processing software kept highlighting these "bad" words warning me, "This language may be offensive to your readers."

"Not my fucking readers!" I banged out on my keyboard. My readers are humorous, intense, curious, and brave passionate warriors!

In these pages, I'm doing what I love, which is supporting you in embracing the gritty humanity of the issues and struggles we all face. This book is me putting my arm around your shoulders, saying, "I'm with you. Let's get in there, unwind yourself, and make shit happen. Let the magic come through."

To get underway, I'll start with some of the hard stuff. If you're curious about what *burning down the house* looks like in my life, it goes like this...

1

DEATH FOR ONE,
REBIRTH FOR ANOTHER

It was a balmy night oh so long ago…
    I had gone out for a drink after work that evening, as I usually did, lying to myself, *just one drink, and I'll be home early*. I had to work the next day. I'd save my worst behavior for the wild weekend to come. Except after a couple of drinks, I was just getting loosened up and losing my sense of time, and as my inhibitions dropped, my intake went up—fast.

I could drink a man twice my size under the table. I was not a simple drinker. I liked the hard stuff. I liked how it burned going down—Southern Comfort right out of the bottle, Mad Dog 20/20 right out of the bottle, gin, vodka, and an endless flow of shots of cinnamon schnapps with tabasco. (Now we're talking!) Cocaine was always a part of it—the white powder blowing my brain to smithereens sobered me up so I could drink more, and cocaine was also my courage. It seemed to remove all my inhibitions that lay between my ears to effortlessly roll off my tongue, as did the alcohol.

I drove home at dawn that morning. I noticed my room-mate and closest friend, Janet, wasn't home. Her motorcycle wasn't in the garage. This was the time she should be eating

7

breakfast before driving off to work. I was concerned, but not enough because I was still high from the cocaine. I focused on trying to sober up - and fast - for work.

In my twenties, at least six nights a week, my friends and I went out dancing or to a bar. I would get off work, shower, and go out to party. Looking back, the word, "party" doesn't seem to fit what we did. The parties started out fun, but eventually, my partying became desperate and soul numbing and out of control. We would snort endless lines of cocaine all night long. I would inevitably throw up on my way to the party, reboot, and rally. I was always throwing up before the escapades, during them, and continuing long into the morning hours.

I spent a lot of time on my knees bowing to the dirty porcelain god of the toilet bowl in bars, in strangers' houses, in gas station bathrooms, and in the bushes as I was walking into the party. As I vomited and the foul taste filled my mouth, I promised that if I could just feel better now, I would stop drinking and drugging for a while—starting tomorrow.

I made endless broken promises to myself that I would not drink or do drugs that night, but it would be the fucking first thing I'd do. Just a few drinks to get rolling—and then find the cocaine.

Janet wasn't home eating breakfast. She wasn't there to pass me in the kitchen well rested and ready for work, it made little sense. She was responsible and punctual. I jumped in the shower to try to sober up, but that didn't help. Coffee. Try to eat something—ugh. There's some yogurt in the refrigerator and an old jar of peanut butter. I dressed in my ill-fitting polyester uniform of dark pants and a red corporate-polyester-issued smock. I wore the ugliest white nursing shoes you've ever seen. They were old, caked, and flaky with so many coats of cheap, white shoe polish they looked like they had leprosy. My shoelaces were ratty on the ends and had basketballs printed on them. Why would I want new shoes when these fit perfectly fine and I was rebellious? I could afford them but would rather spend my money on drugs and booze.

Standing for hours at the register as a grocery checker when you're hungover is not a good feeling. I know because I've done it—a lot. Nauseated. Spinning. Leaning on the counter for support. Trying to look normal. Smelling the booze sweating out of my pores and hoping people around me didn't notice. Feeling the cocaine high turn into a cocaine crash.

Of the ten cashiers, I ranked number one; I checked out more customers per hour with the highest cart value and the least errors. By company standards, I was a high producer, so my boss left me alone most days. If he could tell I was hung-over or zooming on black beauties (speed) a lot of the time, he didn't let on, or perhaps he didn't drink, or drug so couldn't spot the signs. He was a nice guy. I was a fucking mess, very responsible, but a fucking mess, nonetheless.

That morning at home, I had tried all my sobering-up tricks, but I would still be late. I practiced lies looking for one that would be vaguely believable as my newest excuse. As I grabbed my keys, the landline rang. Janet's boss was looking for her, she wasn't at work on time. He didn't want to panic, but knew she rode a motorcycle. I made several calls to friends, but Janet was missing. She never went *missing*. I panicked. Now I had a legitimate excuse for being late. My friend was missing. Should I call the police? Should I call the hospitals or other friends? Just then, the call came from Janet's father. She'd been in a terrible accident —hit by a van on her motorcycle. While I was out partying, a girl who was like a sister to me had ventured out on her motorcycle well after midnight, searching for me, and was now fighting for her life.

I rushed to the hospital and found her in intensive care. Janet was paralyzed from the waist down. Her face was almost unrecognizable—black and blue and swollen. She had a broken jaw, a shattered leg, and was connected to several machines. Her organs had been severely damaged. Three surgeries hadn't stopped the internal bleeding. She was conscious but couldn't speak. She couldn't hold my hand. But when I placed her hand in mine, she moved her finger in my palm in a little scratching motion. She was communicating. What was she trying to tell me? Something in the energy between us let me know she thought everything would be okay, no matter her fate. But the guilt, shame, and sorrow I felt were so deep my tears couldn't touch the level of pain I was in. I can't really explain what was transpiring between us, as if we were communicating in another place and time all together, it was angelic.

I was partying at someone's house while she searched the bars where I was a regular. Janet had been concerned about my whereabouts and ridden her motorcycle thirty miles north trying to find me. As I sat at her bedside, Janet's finger moving inside my palm, I knew she would not make it. I had never been close to the process of death before and had never lost anyone close. Janet died the following day at the age of twenty-two. I made it mean that her body had been destroyed and her life lost—because of me.

Janet was sweet, kind, and she lit up a room. Her very Catholic and conservative parents had disowned her for being gay, which was even more painful to her because Janet had been adopted as a baby and was convinced that she'd been rejected by her birth parents and her adoptive parents. She understood her adoptive parents were people of "faith," but so was she, and her faith made her more loving, not less. Janet prayed and she played Christian music on her guitar—conventional and non-conventional music. Janet loved the band U2 and often sang "I Still Haven't Found What I'm Looking For." After all these years, I still wonder if Janet has found what she was looking for oh so long ago.

She asked me not to say fuck so much. She'd sat at the bathroom door as I got ready to go out again and would quietly suggest that I should consider not going out or drinking for a bit. She did thoughtful things for me I often missed in my self-absorption. She was the salt of earth. She loved me like a sister, even though I didn't love myself, but who does at this age? I assumed we'd go through life as buddies and share it all. And then she was gone.

When two hundred people showed up to mourn her, her parents finally understood how amazing Janet was. It broke their hearts that they had turned their back on her and that so many others had stepped in to honor the beautiful daughter they had disowned. While I gathered in small circles of friends, mourning, inside I felt shameful. *Was this all my fault?* I asked myself over and over.

It was all so complicated. I couldn't process any of it. I avoided feelings by spinning even more out of control, drinking and drugging excessively to numb myself, hoping I'd wake up one day and find she hadn't died. I wanted someone to know the internal turmoil I was in. I drowned my unprocessed emotions by getting fucked up as often and as much as I could. The extra load of shame, guilt, and remorse added to the reasons for my self-harm of excessive drinking and drugging. I was a blackout drinker, and I sometimes woke up in a strange bed, fully clothed with shoes on, with no idea of where I was or the events of the night before. One morning, a friend told me that not only had I drank three bottles of cinnamon schnapps the night before, but I had a pile of cocaine under my nose and face-planted in it. I learned I had also driven my car while being blacked out at least a handful of times. I could have killed someone else, or myself, or both. The shame engulfed me, but I did not stop. Two years passed, and I couldn't remember half of it.

When I had exhausted myself with the subconscious desire to die by self-inflicted behaviors, some little piece of me that wanted to live and be healthy stepped up. I wanted Janet's death to mean something, and it was the catalyst when I was finally ready to be sober at the young age of twenty-five. I turned to Alcoholics Anonymous on February 7th of 1988 after I experienced alcohol poisoning—vomiting violently every fifteen to forty-five minutes for twelve hours straight. It wouldn't be the end of my transformation, but it was a solid beginning. Little did I know back then that it would be the single most important conviction of my lifetime.

Without the drinking and drugging, the emotional pain I had been pushing away engulfed me. It was much worse before it got better. But I kept facing the fear and self-loathing sober. And rather than killing me, the experience of facing the fire again and again scraped my insides clean. I learned life will kill us all. I would learn that love is all that matters. I took responsibility for what was mine and let the rest go.

Over time, I no longer held shame and guilt for a choice that someone else made. This didn't change the reality that I had chosen a reckless self-harming night, and Janet had chosen to look for me. A terrible accident had occurred with Janet on a motorcycle and another person in a van; whose name I do not know, had no doubt suffered lasting repercussions as well. But some relief could come from this tragedy.

With a sober life, mystical experiences would become part of my reality. But that would take much more self-development and was still decades away. First, I had to get sober and stay sober for a long time. The Divine spark was always in me. The first time I felt a power greater than anything I had known before was at the hospital with Janet. Time had seemed to bend. I felt her accept her life and death. I experienced her dignity and surrender. I felt something bigger at work. She had been communicating that all was well, with her hand in mine, and I had heard her.

With sobriety and the study of a variety of wisdom traditions, I've learned we rarely understand the soul contracts of ourselves and of others. It's a bigger mystery than any of us can know fully—but we can touch the mystery. I can love our humanity and accept that things are as they are, knowing that more will be revealed later. This much I know: Janet's death was an initiation for both of us.

I keep a cross of Janet's that is engraved with her name. It's on my altar made of sacred objects that are hanging or in the crevices of a big seven-foot-high piece of Balinese wood that appears to have two bodies merging. These talismans help me remember what it is to turn tragedy into transformation—death to life. Initiations into a new way of BEing are a big deal, and a colorful, created life is full of them. I would like to invite you to fully participate, below, in your creation of a sacred item that honors your journey. List below, as many shameful, guilt-ridden, or remorseful behaviors from the past, and/or present, that you're holding. Vomit it all out, write it all down, and look at it. Feel it. Embrace it. All of it. Cry. Yell. Beat on the sofa. Swing that pillow. Feel It. Let it the fuck out!

When you feel complete with your verbal emotions, close your eyes, and take three slow deep breaths—in through the nose and out through the mouth. Next, get it all down here on paper.

This is FOR you!

Opening the door to setting yourself (and others) free from your self-inflicted feelings.

As they say, "The truth will set you free, but first it will piss you off."

I've allowed for a lot of space for you to fill in over the next few pages.

Use it up.

LET THAT SHIT GO!!

BURNING RITUAL
There is a beautiful burning ritual
for you at the back of this book.
Feel free to go there now,
or when it feels right
for you.
Burn, baby, burn—it!

What happens next involves creating a container to hold your sacred objects. Get creative, use a small shoe box, a wooden box, a tree branch, an apron to sew on an item and use the pockets. Use a vase, a bottle, decorate a jar, use mom's old jewelry box, dad's old tool belt, anything to hold a sacred object, or perhaps your body is the container, and your tattoo is the sacred object—signifying death and rebirth.

How awesome is that? To create something meaningful and sacred, out of self-love. A lived life comes with all sorts of freak accidents, unexpected deaths, illnesses, unimaginable losses, even a global shutdown - who saw that coming?! To create, is to honor ourselves from the inside for the courage and bravery that it took to walk through the situation.

☙ Do you have any photos or memorabilia that signify profound impacts in your life? One's that were painful, yet transformational. (Perhaps you've not gotten to the transformational part yet).

☙ What initiation took place during the worst experiences of your life?

_____

_____

_____

_____

_____

_____

_____

This is for YOU; make a container that brings you joy!
Add your talisman.

2

BORN TO BE WILD

India Zoe Prema looks back at me from the mirror. She has lovely wrinkles around her eyes and mouth from laughing and crying a lot and probably too much sun over the years. She is free, fierce, puts up with nothing, says everything there is to say to anyone she needs to say it to, takes life head on, leads with her heart exposed to the right people at the right time, and is willing to see her shadow and tell the truth about it. Her shadow doesn't frighten her, nor does her light. When life had changed her so much, she had outgrown her former name, and just like clockwork, Spirit dropped her current name right in! The name of a country and the Indus River that runs through it.

When one of her tattoos outlives its usefulness as a symbol of transformation, she has it covered in new ink that tells her new story. She offers grace to her teaching and moves on. She cares what the people she loves and respects think about her, but everyone else – not so much! Why would she care what you think when you know absolutely nothing about her? Ahh, control, judgement, arrogance—that's where humanity sits in its shadow. To empathize or understand another, you must first swim in the same waters that drowned them.

India was born to be free—in a good way—that took her decades to understand. She can camp in the dirt as easily as she can sleep in the comfort of her organic bed or in a five-star hotel. She strides into a room with her head held high and lives from the inside out. She's sober, organized, centered, knows how to get things done, lives well in a beautiful home, but being comfortable in life doesn't mean she's arrived at her final destination. She's wild but tamed. She loves deeply and serves those who need her—with passion. She doesn't suffer fools—at all.

When India's death shows up, however it arrives, whenever it arrives—as an illness, old age, or an 18-wheeler barreling down upon her—she'll surrender fully, saying, "Wow. Thank you! What a great fucking life!"

*

Now what about the woman named Cheryl Joanne Duncan? India would have scared Cheryl shitless once upon a time. Her insecurity, lack of any hardships, deficient in so many experiences, yet she judged from the fringes of it all. Something about India would seem a bit too *much* for Cheryl; India had lived a life she had not.

But that was before the refiner's fire beat and forged Cheryl Joanne Duncan like a Samurai sword on the anvil of life so she could die to herself repeatedly to be reborn. She found a new name and a new life as India Zoe Prema.

Cheryl took everything seriously and judged from a place she never visited. India laughs even at the tragedies she's experienced and says she wouldn't change one thing to be where she is now. Cheryl's limited beliefs held her in self-bondage. She was a martyr and riddled with anger underneath it all. She was self-sacrificing because anything else would be selfish.

Cheryl saw herself as the *victim of circumstances* and justified her *shit storms* again and again. She spent hours looping in stories about those who had *harmed her* and had no capacity to know that she was sad or hurt and, therefore, lived in anger and resentment. She gave away her power while trying to control everything. She didn't feel comfortable in her own skin. While appearing kind on the surface, Cheryl had a limited capacity for feeling compassion for others, unable to relate to their circumstances or their choices. Underneath the niceness was a fearful, defensive ego. This part of her was calling the shots; while she was kind to others, she was really a little shit.

Cheryl lived from the outside in. At the unconscious level, she was scrambling to make it all look good to others because what others thought mattered more to her than her own experience. Cheryl had a successful career and good standing in the community. She was an alcoholic & addict in recovery, adept at the Steps & Traditions and sponsoring others in Alcoholics Anonymous. She had lots of lovely possessions: a nice car, a high credit score, a sweet California bungalow in a nice neighborhood two blocks from the Pacific Ocean, and money in the bank. Her identity was wrapped up in the comfortable blanket of her limited comfort zone. Life was working just as she designed it.

From the outside, it all seemed perfect. The future looked so bright she had to wear shades. And then this comfortable life slipped through her fingers—all at once—and was gone, just gone, as if it never existed. Leaving her raw, vulnerable, and exposed.

☙ Where in your life have you felt raw, vulnerable, or exposed?

———————————————————————————

———————————————————————————

———————————————————————————

_____

_____

_____

_____

☙ Has your need for worldly possessions covered up your feelings of emptiness, lack of self-worth, or self-esteem? If so, how? If not, is it possible that you may have a blind-spot here? If you aren't sure what this means – ask yourself, "who would I be or who am I without all the stuff: the title, the money, the neighborhood, the cars, etc."

_____

_____

_____

_____

_____

_____

_____

☙ When your final day comes, will you be able to say, "Wow. Thank you! What a great fucking life!" Or will you feel regret?

🔥 What has made it a great life, or what will you regret?

_____

_____

_____

_____

_____

_____

_____

🔥 Is there something new to discover about how you've told
the story of your life? How so?

_____

_____

_____

_____

_____

_____

_____

3

WHAT THE FUCK DID WE DO?!

December 19, 2004 was a day of switching lives, time zones, and temperatures, with even more change than I could have imagined waiting just around the corner to whack me—hard. The day began on an unusually hot morning in Long Beach, California, but it was pitch dark in the late night as I stood on frozen ground in Charlotte, North Carolina, a flurry of snowflakes dancing about me with my little family huddled inside our freezing new home. My partner, Dawson, and I had moved across the country that day, and that was a big change. We had considered our options carefully and planned everything down to the last detail because if you control *everything*, it all works *perfectly*.

During our seventeen-year partnership, the decisions Dawson and I made were centered around the quality of our local Alcoholics Anonymous community. In our AA (Alcoholics Anonymous) meetings in Long Beach, we felt our first level of responsibility was to the newcomer, and the second level was to the visitor. You need to be there for others because you never know if someone from out-of-town might be on a business trip, visiting family, in deep distress, about to relapse, or on the lam. That's how we measured a place, by the solidity of their AA.

22

I'd tiptoe to my computer before dawn and ramble around, looking for interesting possibilities online. I went wilder even looking at listings for property in places around the world. An organic coffee farm in Costa Rica? I tried on all sorts of imagined futures, wondering where we could build a new life. Options outside the U.S. didn't seem to fit us at the time, so my search refocused on the United States. And for what appeared to be an odd reason at the time, I was drawn and pulled to the South. And to my knowledge, we had zero family history east of Indiana.

When Dawson and I traveled for work or pleasure, we'd break out the directory of AA meetings and hit the biggest meeting we could find. While seeking and visiting three other possibilities for relocation, we partook in the big meetings in Portland, Austin, or Rochester. We were not given a warm welcome after identifying ourselves as "visitors," therefore, not meeting our standards of sobriety. We decided on the adventure of a place we didn't know—Charlotte, North Carolina.

Charlotte was a dart-on-the-map destination. We only knew one person there. Dawson had sponsored a woman named Krystal in AA, and when Krystal moved back to her hometown of Charlotte, she became our local connection. Krystal assured us that if we settled there, we'd have a place in an AA community that aligned with us. That we would be met with open arms and strong sobriety. I didn't realize it at the time, but how we chose to live and participate in our sobriety was to judge those who did not live in the same reflection as we did.

We leaned into the adventure. A long-time lesbian couple would leave queer-friendly Long Beach and head for the Bible-belt, NASCAR South. What could possibly go wrong?

While looking for a home, we drove the green hills of this subtropical climate and just thirty miles north of Charlotte, discovered Lake Norman, where there was more space, peace, and quiet. We jumped in quickly and purchased a beautiful home on an acre of land and within forty-five days moved across country.

Before leaving Los Angeles permanently, a place I called home since the day I was born, I met one last time with a psychic medium who was the most "woo-woo" person I'd known at that point. Jeannie connected with guides, angels, ancestors, and used cards in her readings. I'd been seeing her for years, at first scratching my head at it all, but by then, I knew she was onto something. She connected to energies beyond three-dimensional reality. But instead of feeling reverence or being intrigued, I still treated the experience like it was a novelty; a side show at the carnival, not as the important spiritual communication it was.

Jeannie was astounded when I turned over five rebirthing cards. I was so arrogant and naïve. I thought I was going to finally get what I deserved: more money, a big title, extended wealth, accolades, you fucking name it! At the time, I thought these cards meant all those things would be gifted to me, I would finally be seen in, "all my glory." Unbeknownst to me, those five angel cards represented my future adventures that gave me more deaths and rebirths than I can count, and several are represented in these pages.

Our departure out of Los Angeles to Charlotte was a literal shit show with our two small dogs, Ruby and Oliver, and our cat, Mochi, in separate carriers. We knew Mochi would bolt hard if she had a chance. As a security guard inspected the animals, he accidentally opened the door of the carrier a bit too much, and Mochi took off like a rocket. How could anyone possibly catch a cat running around an airport? Dawson had a split second to make the call; she tackled the cat, throwing her body over Mochi. But Mochi bit Dawson on the hand, and now there was blood everywhere. Think of this mess at the airport like an episode of "I Love Lucy," and we're playing the parts of Lucy and Ethel, wrangling a cat and two dogs across the country.

During our flight, Dawson was hunched over a vomit bag because of horrible motion sickness caused by inner ear damage as a baby. Our wobbly, nauseated, and wounded family circus arrived in Charlotte late on a cold night, exhausted and frozen because the furnace wasn't working in our new home. Our breath was visible in the house, and the animals were confused and probably wondering what the fuck was going on. *What is this cold, unfamiliar place?*

Dawson and I bundled up in layers, wrapping ourselves and the beasts in whatever we had available to try to keep warm. And it was uncomfortably quiet. The cold and isolated silence of the country made me nervous. My head was running a-muck. *People go missing or die out here when it's so quiet and isolated.* As I flopped onto the queen-size blow-up mattress with flannel sheets, my head barely hit my pillow, and I heard a car, with no tailpipes, on the backside of our isolated home, I started crying and said to Dawson, "What the fuck did we do?"

As Dawson and I settled into our new home and community, I continued working for the same company in Long Beach. Within two months, I was hired by a global staffing firm to manage the most profitable branch in North America. My first sixty days were grueling. I needed to build my team of three employees to a team of nine, all while needing a Ph.D. in psychiatry to deal with the three I inherited when I was hired. Within six months, I was being sought after by other companies and interviewed with them; I needed out of my job, which had quickly become emotionally toxic.

One of my skills is preparing people to effectively interview for a high-level corporate positions. I was a high-level recruiter, for God's sake! I made an excellent living matching highly compensated people and my clients' positions. But here I was, sabotaging each opportunity as I made the rounds of companies in Charlotte. I was behaving like someone who didn't know better. I would walk away from a job possibility asking, *Why did I do that? Why did I say that? Why did I seem so disengaged?* It was such odd behavior for me that nothing made sense. Something was off, but I wouldn't have been able to tell you what or why for many years to come. But at that time, I was wandering around bitter and pissed off— even though I was the one doing the sabotaging. I was not outward with those feelings; rather, I held them in—tightly. I was composed mostly, even when fueled. And since those feelings had nowhere to go, they all went straight to anger, and that too was held in until the wrong moment hit. Then I barked, and I barked loudly.

And when it doesn't work out perfectly, do you suffer from feeling as though you're not getting what you want? I did. And I say this from being on one side of that delusion to being on the other side of it: We don't know what we don't know, until we do! We look into the crazy things we do to avoid ourselves to live in our chaos.

Now that I have expressed my emotional immaturity in so many ways, let's identify some of the ways you too may have areas of improvement.

֍ Where in your life do you hold anger, resentment or entrap others into your web so you feel more empowered?

_____

_____

_____

_____

_____

_____

_____

_____

_____

_____

_____

_____

❦ Jot down some notes about major turning points in your life where you (seemingly) sabotaged yourself. At the time, did it feel you were undermining yourself? Were you baffled by your behavior? Did you take yourself down a bad road of beating yourself up? Yah, me too!

_____

_____

_____

_____

_____

_____

_____

_____

_____

_____

_____

And here's a thought, *We are often being led by the Universe to course correct. It's when we don't course correct that it gets painful. Subsequently, we see that something has happened* to *us, but it's* always *happening* for *us.* I didn't always see it that way either—until my inner journey unfolded so deeply that I was brought to my knees more than once.

🔥 Where in your life do you see things are happening *to* you and not *for* you? (*To* you keeps you in the "victim" space)

_____

_____

_____

_____

_____

_____

_____

_____

_____

_____

_____

_____

_____

_____

_____

_____

❦ Where in your current life could you course correct? Meaning, making changes to things that are not working for you? (Examples may include, your job, a relationship, or patterns of behavior)

_____

_____

_____

_____

_____

_____

_____

_____

_____

_____

_____

_____

_____

_____

_____

The clearer you are about seeing these events in your past, the more you'll gain awareness of your present and the ability to shape your future.

4

ADDICTED TO DRAMA

Judging success from the outside, we had landed on our feet and were re-creating our perfect little world again. In Charlotte, we had a few great neighbors who were from all over the country. Our new AA home group was just right; our physical home was beautiful and cost half as much as our home in Long Beach and was four times the size. In Charlotte, we had hardwood floors, ten-foot ceilings, and a great room larger than our entire home had been.

I finally quit sabotaging myself, found a good-paying job, and was earning the same amount of money I had made in California. Dawson was charging the same rates for acupuncture, so we were prosperous. This would lead to an inflated sense of self and a string of bad decisions. But that wasn't everything that was going on. Let's talk about the shame of a nation—let's talk about racism.

Our first year in the South showed us how different it was from Southern California. People were friendly, kind, and respectful, but in the American South, I learned the visceral truth about systemic racism and how it infused into everything and was found everywhere. White families, who had homes for generations, passed inherited wealth to the next generation, thinking that was the natural order of things.

Families who had the opportunity to seek good schools and higher education and had the funds for it, and had for generations, were unaware of the grinding struggle of families who descended from ancestors for whom even learning to read meant risking death at the end of a noose. So why had I placed myself in the middle of all this? I think it was because I was ready to garner some new teaching life obliged. However, I was just pissed off at everyone in the South for all the injustices, and then I become righteous about it.

I had probably always been much more sensitive to the energies of places and people than I'd realized. There was something energetically off about the vibration that I was experiencing in my body and soul in Charlotte. I was vibrating all the time at a low energetic frequency, and it wasn't a good thing. I could sense, see, and connect with the pain, suffering, cruelty, and violent deaths that had occurred during the genocide of native tribes, throughout the history of slavery, the civil war, the Jim Crow laws, and the aftermath of suffering that is still playing out on that soil and in the lineage of people and their families.

If you've been to such places, you may know what I mean by being able to *feel* this history and how it shows up in the present. The racism is still there in racist places with names that haven't been changed. It's as if time literally stopped.

At another point in time, I had hired and relocated Dawn, an African American woman, from the big city of Philadelphia to rural Arkansas. I had established a deep relationship with her as our vendor consultant over a two-year period. As we were out to lunch one afternoon, she said she wanted to experience all the nature Arkansas and Louisiana had to offer: bayous, hot springs, Ozarks, bicycling, and camping. "I will take you anywhere you want to go and experience - but not camping!" "I am not taking a black person out into the woods anywhere in the South!" It was so painful to say that to someone, and at the same time, I am so grateful that my friendships, in all their colors, can be so honest and transparent. And yet, I was angry I even had to say it.

The confederate flag was flown proudly, and when people shouted, "The South Will Rise Again!" They absolutely did not mean *rise unified to face and heal our excruciating past.* The pain of the past and present was in the very air I breathed, in the water, and in the soil. And I felt it all.

As much as I burned myself out, I'm so grateful for this experience. How else would I have learned that I was energetically sensitive in this way, unless I was in a place that precisely pushed *those* buttons? How could I overcome the anger that descended on me and engulfed me when I saw the systemic racism of a nation on full display? I had to live in a place like this to learn there is no such thing as neutrality. If we're not a part of the solution, we're a part of the problem. And we must face our shortcomings and solve them, in our individual lives, as families, as communities, as cultures, and as humanity.

*

I never set myself on a conscious path of change. How could I? And why would I? But it was revealed to me, many years later, that it was necessary for me to experience some of the pain and wounds of others, in order to transform the suffering. The change in me would eventually happen, as I had to do a great deal of work on myself to develop the tools to transform. Eventually, I would mature into a woman who could go deep with people to support them on their journey to Self-discovery. But during the time we lived in Charlotte, I didn't know what I was called to do, so I could only feel pain and wounds. I didn't even know how to speak of it—this empathetic pain and anger. And I didn't know what I could do to heal it in myself and others, so it enveloped me, smothering any joy and leaving me to continuously burn in my indignation.

I was so fucking angry that all I could think about when I saw black families who had lived there for generations was, *How can you even function in this society with the amount of anger you must be carrying?* I saw how so many white families, businesses, and institutions had benefitted from slavery and ongoing racism for almost three centuries—yes, *three centuries*! Did they pretend not to know the truth of the source of their wealth? Or did they really not even know? Did they carry shame buried deep under all that self-justification? I could not wrap my head around how fucked up it all was. Didn't white people get it? Weren't they committed to trying to understand someone else's experience while unable to ever walk in their shoes?

Our beliefs and emotional states impact our behavior. My actions arced in a downward spiral in part because I didn't have the tools to process this historical trauma and turn it into the right action. I could have found a community taking on the issues I cared about and made my contribution along with them. I could have found those who were working to bring economic, social, gender, and racial justice to the region and leaning hard into the challenge of making a difference. If I had done that, my time in Charlotte would have been very different. Instead, I wallowed in my drama and didn't end up accomplishing anything I could point to as making a difference in that place.

I was also asleep spiritually. I saw life only from ordinary 3-D reality. I didn't know what it is like to be part of something magical that happens at higher energetic frequencies.

What would it take to wake me up spiritually or to know any self-awareness? Experiences so profound they couldn't be denied.

Ready to take this on with me? Let's go. But first let's look at where you are hooked by your story in unhealthy drama, where your anger burns without creating anything. They say we can either complain or create, but not both, at the same time. If you aren't in action, get in action. If you need to speak up, speak up. If there is something to do other than complain, sign up and roll up your sleeves. If something sucks, work to un-suck it!

Do you have the right to complain about the state of a nation if you don't vote—unless you just like to complain, bitch, and moan?

And away we go...

   Complaining offers a false sense of self, whereas creating offers a truer sense of your essence, authenticity, joy, and love. Where in your life do you complain and become self-righteous instead of participating in right action?

_____

_____

_____

_____

_____

_____

_____

If we can only choose one—complaining or creating—
which one do you generally choose? _____
Why?

HINT: It's doing something *for* you, that's why. What is
that something? What is it covering up that is lacking within
you (self-worth, confidence, self-esteem, security, etc.)?

_____

_____

_____

_____

_____

_____

The biggest addiction, in my humble opinion, is drama.
It's a damn blowtorch that will set us on a course of annihilation and destroy everything in its path, especially the path
of relationships—with both self and others.

   ê   Where does your anger burn you to a cinder rather than
      create a fire in your belly for change?

_____

_____

_____

_____

_____

_____

❧ Let your inner drama (queen or king) finish these sentences.
- I'm not responsible for...
- I never...
- They always...
- If I don't do this, nobody will...
- What did I do to deserve all this?
- It's not fair that...
- I'm entitled to...
- It's not my fault, it's....
- Why does _____ always happen to *me*?!

Drama is focused on the ego self and will fry everyone around you, unless they, too, operate within the drama.

5

BURN, BABY, BURN

Have you felt left out, judged unfairly, thwarted, ignored, or misunderstood? These are experiences that challenge us to work it out on the inside first before engaging outside of ourselves with others. But that's difficult because it can seem as if we're going along minding our own business, and then something happens that others *do to us*, and we *react* to what we imagine is the thing that *triggers* us. That's how it seems, but life mastery is an inside-out job. That can be hard to see in all our circumstances.

Because of the color of our skin, Dawson and I fit in with certain people in the South until they found out we weren't just best friends or roommates, but we were the dreaded species—gay. I was born and raised in Los Angeles, and I dressed in my creativity. I wore my chocolate-colored business suit with a fuchsia-colored top and artsy-fartsy butterscotch-colored glasses, and this self-expression alone was enough to throw people sideways. I didn't act like a local or look like one. I was constantly stared at and (inappropriately and unconsciously) questioned. "Darlin', you're not from around these parts, are yoouuuu?" Those words, any words when used in this tone and context, are often spoken to us from a place of judgement, criticism, or fear, as opposed to curiosity, intrigue, or fascination. How does the colorful way that someone chooses to express themselves have anything to do with who they are? Is there integrity lessened, their character shortened, or their humanity non-existent because their clothes aren't to your style?

I was in the same profession as men who looked at me and spoke down to me as if I belonged barefoot and pregnant in the kitchen. I could simply feel it, and eventually validated and confirmed it with my female friends who were born and raised in Charlotte.

Misogyny and bigotry toward queer people are baked into American culture. The roots of both run deep. But until our time in North Carolina, I was accustomed to bigotry and misogyny rearing their ugly heads almost never. It didn't mean it didn't exist in LA; rather, it was not my personal experience. In Charlotte, the obvious bad treatment we faced was out in the open, and it permeated many interactions. There was a hierarchy. Race the major factor, gender and sexuality were right there, too. And we'd better know our place.

Now I scratch my head about those who live in the intersection of those bigotries. What do black gay men and women face? Black trans people? Their reality is often a dangerous one. For us, as a mated pair of white gay women, it was more of an aggravating circumstance, and I went into my storytelling of how fucked up it all was; therefore, I continued to take part in the problem and not in any solutions; I was only inconvenienced. I was also judging and criticizing the complete lack of self-awareness in others and could not see my own lack of awareness. We always think it's them! Funny how that works!

Spraying blanket quotes, tags, and statements such as "Stop racism" or "We're all in this together" or "Inspire change" in the endzone of a football field means nothing if there is no self-work, or self-awareness, that helps and supports individuals in understanding their blind-spots. Without this attention to self, these displays become smoke and mirrors.

I would spend months on the job building client relationships and creating genuine rapport, taking people out to lunch, really listening, and gathering information about their business needs—that was my role. Time and time again, just when we were in the flow, I'd get the question in a honey Southern drawl, "So, Ms. Cheryl, why did you and your huuuusband move to Charlotte?" When I shared—with honesty, authenticity, and integrity—that I didn't have a man, but a woman whom I had been with for 13 years, they hid their shock and surprise. And that client never worked with me again.

As I was expressing myself to a dear friend of ours one day, she shared with me that her therapist had told her and her husband, "Even having a *friendship* with those two women is *morally wrong!*" I had no words. A realtor showed us a potential location for Dawson's acupuncture business, but once he found out we were life partners and not business partners, he never showed us another property or returned any of our calls. We had several contractors come to the house to do work, but when they learned there was no "man of the house," they didn't return. These experiences propelled my downward spiral because I took on the drama of the situation. But what did I expect when we moved there? Really. What fantasy was I spinning that brought on personal suffering when these good ol' boys didn't show up flying rainbow flags? I knew they wouldn't. So why be so surprised? I suffered in drama-queen territory for certain.

I chose to be alienated by this bigotry. I chose not to find my footing in this place. I chose to suffer and be immature rather than be empowered by the circumstances I/we had put ourselves in on purpose, even though we lacked the understanding of this.

I experienced anger, anger, anger. I cycled between three ways of being angry—low grade pissed off, growing anger burning in the furnace, then triggered to full blown, volcanic rage. Anger is great when it's channeled to fuel transformation, breakthroughs, and positive action. Anger for its own sake can burn us to a crisp if it doesn't move through us. My anger was burning hot and unproductive; I was volatile and crisp as crackling, that's the Southern delicacy of deep-fried pork skin. That's how I felt. And that's how I behaved. Crackling. Burning in the fire.

Are you ready to burn into *your* fire…

❧ My anger was burning hot and unproductive. "I was volatile and as crisp as crackling." Can you relate to this? (Painful, I know.)
   Is yours? How so?

_____

_____

_____

_____

_____

❧ When have you felt that you've been treated unfairly, disrespected, or looked down upon?

_____

_____

_____

_____

_____

❦ What does this bring up in you?

_____

_____

_____

_____

❦ Are there circumstances in your life that could fuel meaningful change if you have the courage to walk through
the fire?

_____

_____

_____

_____

❦ Are there experiences in your life in which you choose to
remain in the drama or toxicity of your behavior, fanning
those flames repeatedly? How about we get those bad boys
out here on paper?

_____

_____

_____

_____

❦ How does remaining here serve you?

_____

_____

_____

_____

6

HIDING, PUFFING, AND COVERING UP

To share my life with vulnerability and absolute honesty took time. For decades, I would not have exposed myself as I'm about to for you—in living color.

I would never have talked about what it was like as a child to worry about the power being disconnected because we couldn't pay the bill, or what it felt like when the refrigerator was nearly empty and a certain, quiet panic set in. While I did not have a formal education, I relied upon my common sense, my intuition; I even followed the energy, even though I didn't understand anything about it until several decades later.

I had this inherent sense of knowing things, but I did not understand why or how I knew what I did. It's a sense of knowing that I couldn't explain, and I wouldn't know there was such a thing called *claircognizant* for many years to come.

At thirty-two, I was tasked to be a project manager on a massive project that required a team of six to eight people. I had two, me included. I was responsible for managing a client's project and seven million dollars of corporate office furniture that included 968 cubicles, 12 training rooms, 64 hard wall offices, 23 conference rooms of various sizes, and

1,500 chairs with custom fabric. It was an unprecedented project of high visibility in the Silicon Valley. My ability to manage so many moving parts and anticipate where shit could go wrong and course correct was beyond anyone's comprehension, including myself. I just knowingly knew what to do. I didn't lose a penny out of that seven million, and I got a nice raise because of it!

Having these incredible gifts show up in my life, and not knowing or understanding all that I do now, only caused me and others frustration. Others saw me as overbearing, and I, in return, saw them as short-sighted and incompetent. I hadn't yet understood that I was operating from my ego. Because that that sense of knowing was so strong, and it never led me astray, I would push my agenda on others. I would get so frustrated with people who only saw one slice of the pie or only what was right in front of them, which would ultimately lead to mistakes. I, however, could see the whole pie, which included any mishaps that could arise, and I could easily see what not to do, in order to have a clean outcome. "Shit in. Shit out," as I say.

I had lots of tricks for trying to feel safe and important in the world. Money was one of my favorite ways to show how successful I had become without a college degree. Many people hide behind money if they have it. *Look at what I wear and drive and where I go and how I live! See. I'm financially successful; I am worthy!*

Our society emphasizes the value of a person based on their earning power, therefore, leaving many people who don't have money to feel inadequate and insecure. All the while, they're judging those who have money, as they burn with desire for it. And millions spend money they don't have until they are indentured servants to banks and credit card companies. The way people mangle and tangle money into their self-esteem and insecurity has many variations. I know because I've done all of it.

My parents had just enough money to survive when I was growing up. They struggled to put food on the table for my two brothers and me. Five of us lived in a two-bedroom apartment. I slept on the floor in the living room from the age of three until six, when my parents bought a little bed that we put against the wall in our tiny kitchen. We had powdered milk, puffed rice cereal, bread from the day-old bakery, and dented canned goods that had been marked down. It was not the most well-balanced and nutritious diet, but most of the time, we could eat.

My mom worked two jobs while my dad was in law school. Both my parents were busy day and night, and my two older brothers didn't give me the time of day because a little girl wasn't interesting to them, so I spent a lot of time alone not feeling connected to anyone. I wondered where my actual family was because this group of people made no sense to me.

Our entire apartment was 800 square feet, so whenever I got in trouble and didn't have a bedroom to be banished to, the joke in the family was, "Go to your closet, Cheryl." I didn't really go to my closet, but rather to my parents' small bedroom. I was searching for some connection to the people I lived with, and when I wasn't getting attention, I acted out. I was seeking attention of any kind from anyone. Throughout my life, my mom always shared with me that my dad would tell her she needed to do something with me, as I was too independent; I was three! I was raised in the era of, "Be seen and not heard," and as a girl, what was expected of me was a much higher standard than my brothers.

But the gift of being alone was honing the skill of independence. Even as early as three years of age, I could handle being alone and taking care of myself. As I grew up, I became sporty, playing softball and every after-school sport there was, in order to have some control over my circumstances. I got good at things; that's where I felt my value. And my value got connected to performance and money.

As a teenager, I would steal a dollar or two about once a week from my dad's wallet, which he kept in a desk drawer, and I did a fair share of stealing from my mom—her cigarettes, she was a closet smoker (a bathroom-blowing-smoke-out-the-window smoker…followed by half a can of Lysol). I didn't feel bad about stealing from my parents, I justified and rationalized my behavior since my parents never had money, subsequently, I never got an allowance or had money to go do things, not even see a movie, and by the age of twelve, I just did what I wanted until I possibly got caught - which I never did. But morally, that was where I started to draw the line for myself.

I had no college education, no inheritance, no scholarship, no certainty, no free money, and nothing financial had been handed to me. The total financial gifts my parents could afford to give me, beyond the food, clothing, and shelter of my childhood, was $500 total. This includes the $200 my mom gave me with a card on my 40th birthday.

Once I was finally sober and had more clarity, and *in order to* cover up my deep *insecurity and lack of any self-worth*, I worked hard to build financial *security*. I considered myself a bit of a financial expert. I worked and worked until I had everything I needed and wanted. Pat on the back. Smug feeling of superiority. If others didn't have it, it was because they didn't have the backbone to earn it. This is what I believed at the time—it was so unconscious.

To compensate for the *belief* that I was not enough, I was an overachiever at work and in most areas of my life. I strived for excellence and took pleasure and pride in creating something from nothing. While it brought me joy, it also covered up a crack in my foundation where self-worth was missing.

Puffing up and hiding our insecurities – our low self-esteem – to seem more significant and more admirable, is part of the human condition. We all want to be seen, heard, and respected, so we contort ourselves into many strange positions to achieve that which we are lacking within ourselves. This is also part of the human condition that is unaware – our shadow, our blind spots.

*

I am highly efficient, and laser focused, so I get a lot done. Dawson often said, "If you did fifty percent less, you would still do more than most people and still as good a job." I liked those kinds of compliments. They were like catnip for my ego, but I still didn't understand what she meant. Low self-worth and low self-esteem can be dressed up in a fancy package. Mine was competence.

Dawson had two master's degrees, one in kinesiology and one in Chinese Medicine. I wanted her to be proud of me and to be proud to be with me as her partner. My success at the time and the thing that made me feel valuable was money. But what I didn't know about money would sneak up and side swipe me. If my competence turned into incompetence, then who would I be? What I feared most, being a "loser," would cause me to lose my fragile sense of self. So, here's how I lost:

I had been clever about paying off all substantial debt—my remaining school loan from my associate degree, Dawson's second master's degree, and my car—with a nicely organized spreadsheet of credit cards, moving the debt around to 0% cards and paying it off with discipline. I loved the organization of our finances. It was tidy. We kept our word. We paid on time or early. We made good money. Because it all had gone well for several years, we felt it should go this way forever. We believed we deserved good luck to roll downhill and end up at our front door—continuously. But underneath, I was wrapped up in financial fear, overwhelmed, trying to control people, places, and things; basically trying to control every damned thing down to the last cent.

*

Back to the American South, it's 2005; I was working for a company in Charlotte for just nine months and found myself emotionally spent. I looked for a quick and easy way to get out of what I now saw as the corporate rat race. I had fond memories of working to spruce properties up with my parents. They had become realtors who dreamed of living in a house like the ones they sold. They never quite got there, but when we worked on a home together as a family, our sweat equity was fueled by hope. The hope we could "make it." I turned to real estate to make my break from corporate employment and expand my financial success.

I embraced real estate after my first big win in 2005, setting the ball in motion for my "real-estate empire." My first win felt like a high, like people who are addicted to gambling and often experience that feeling on an early win. This only distorts reality; it came easy and fast, then they chase that easy fix, even if they lose everything and live on the street panhandling to buy a lottery ticket. Well, that first big win in 2005 – that was my big "high," so I greased the skids of my downfall by making fast, easy purchases.

While Dawson was on a backpacking trip on the Appalachian Trail with some friends, I jumped in to surprise her by wholesaling my first property, which means I found an abandoned and distressed piece of real-estate and found the buyer who was a fit for it. I got a fee without even paying for the property, getting a cut from the deal I put together. When Dawson returned home, I had the check in my hand,

$12,000 for a small amount of time invested. At first, she didn't believe me when I shared the fun news, then she also caught the fever of easy money.

Being accustomed to real estate prices in Los Angeles, we were astounded at the relatively inexpensive property we could purchase in North Carolina. Like pirates plundering on the open sea, we couldn't get enough. In our determined mindset, we purchased several properties from a wholesaler. Every property had major issues; therefore, we kept them, since we couldn't flip them for the easy money they originally *penciled out* to. So, we decided there was nothing for us to do but keep them and manage the properties with their insurmountable problems.

There was no grace, compassion or kindness in our little real estate empire, only self-justification, immaturity, entitlement, and me flipping out—which I did regularly. General contractors didn't show up or get necessary permits. Inspections weren't honest. We didn't vet tenants properly, and when they didn't pay and squatted for months on end, our losses mounted. Demolition went wrong, contractors and inspectors who said they had insurance didn't have insurance, people I thought of as friends scammed us by dumping problem properties on us, and we made loan payments on properties that sat empty waiting for contractors. Thieves broke in to steal everything and anything that could be sold or traded for drugs: copper piping, HVACs, windows, doors, and appliances.

But wait, there's more! Within a few days of putting a "For Sale by Owner" sign up on a property located on Bond Street, there was a badly beaten prostitute's body thrown, literally thrown, onto the front yard! She was discovered the next morning by contractors. It was horrific—on so many levels. It was plastered all over the front page of the local newspaper.

I don't know how I didn't have a nervous breakdown. Maybe I did, I don't know...

Breathe.
Just Breathe.
Just Breathe.
But I couldn't.

While that painful experience was unfolding, there was another unfolding right on top of it. A property with mold in the basement led to the discovery that this hazardous problem was caused by a natural spring that flowed under the house. Try getting a bid for rerouting a spring flowing under a house to the tune of $13,800. The easy money we were chasing brought more problems and no solutions.

Another one of our houses was literally collapsing around its foundation because the termite infestation was much bigger than anyone realized. The termite house was the collateral for a loan—short term, high interest and generally used for rehabbing and flipping real-estate. Therefore, we could not tear the house down and rebuild. We had no other option but to have the joist and foundation replaced while the entire house was sitting on it. Finding a contractor willing to do this kind of very risky work was not easy or cheap. The total cost to replace the entire band seal and joist was $35,000. Now we're looking at almost $50,000 on two properties. Even if we could have sold the property, we would have taken a hefty loss. The anger that continuously suffocated me only worsened. I couldn't breathe with all the smoke and mirrors I'd created in my life. Failure would mean I was not competent, and competence was the part of me I solely relied upon.

Over the next several months, we had a few opportunities to purchase additional wholesale properties, and again, we didn't take the time to perform due diligence because they were bargains that needed to be snapped up quickly. Our over-zealousness and bad judgement bit us on the ass a few more times in the next several months. We purchased two additional properties as a package, only to find out after the transaction was complete, that we did not own half of the front yard across both houses. The realtor who was wholesaling them failed to disclose this. Our insurance didn't cover any of this nonsense.

A lack of integrity all around meant plenty of blame to share. The financial blows were striking harder and harder. The more they landed, the more my fears about money were rearing their ugly heads. The fury inside me felt like a gas leak waiting for someone to strike a match.

I was still not listening,
Not listening,
Not listening.

How could I when I had no idea, understanding, or knowledge that these were some of my teachings, so I just fought back. Not an ounce of surrender in sight!

One of these problems would have been enough, but we had created so many at once, and I was emotionally immature. I lost my shit multiple times a day, every day. I trusted people who should not have been trusted because I was afraid to see the truth and preferred my made-up version of reality to what was really there. I was a headstrong, entitled jackass, and an overbearing victim, hoping to be rescued from the saga I created. Everything was everybody else's fault. I experienced life from a place of, "You'd be this pissed off too if all this shit was happening to you!" I was attracting drama after drama and pushing through, as if there was a way through. And the messes compounded—with interest.

On one very-pissed-off day, disassociated and not in my body, I drove away from the fuel pump at a gas station with the nozzle still attached to my car. I drove until the hose nearly snapped. I skidded to a stop, got out of my car, replaced the hose in the slot, and tried to play it off as the cool, calm, and collected queen bee that I was. But I knew I could have blown things up. *Fuck, fuck, fuck.*

I felt as if I was in my own warzone; the responsibility of holding seven mortgages is no joke. The depth of my attachment to money, my anger, drama addiction, and my need to maintain control continued to bite me on the ass for the next several years. I believed, *We've sacrificed to have blah blah blah* and, *We've earned what we have blah blah blah*, and I was hanging on by bleeding fingertips with the thought, *This is rightly ours.* I was self-righteous, holier than thou, and it never occurred to me, due to lack of self-awareness, I was the beginning point to ending the madness.

I had the underlying fear of ending up living under a bridge, drinking rot-gut booze out of a paper bag, and dying there alone. This story of my imagined bag-lady future played over and over in my mind day and night. The financial mess was presenting a big lesson—but I wasn't having any part of learning it! How could I? When all I had known until then was to believe the *irrational fears I created in my mind and, ultimately, live by them.*

My ego loved to distill it into something so simple; *it was everyone else's fault.* I knew I'd hit rock bottom when I heard these words come out of my mouth, flying towards squatters in one of our properties. I literally yelled "I am going to burn this motherfucking house down to the ground, and I hope to hell you're not in it!" That's how out of control and in my shadow I was.

I could not find the teaching, the medicine, or the gift in our real estate misadventure to save my life; though I had no idea what that meant at the time. All I could see was that everything was happening *to* me, and nothing ever *for* me.

Other than seeking the external validation of material success, I had no practical tools, no language, no spiritual reference points to measure the value of my existence. I was measuring it all from outside of myself, just as we're all taught.

Let's take a moment to reflect on how you're measuring your own life. Is it from the inside or the outside? To know where you're going, it's good to know where you currently stand.

๖ What's your relationship with money? Is it inspiring or frightening?

_____

_____

_____

_____

๖ How do you currently identify your *Self*-value?

_____

_____

_____

_____

๖ Who do you compare yourself to and feel inferior or superior to in secret?

_____

_____

_____

_____

❧ What do you do to seek approval and admiration of others? Who are these others you want to impress?

_____

_____

_____

_____

❧ What are you trying to control about your life's circumstances? Who do you try to control and why?

_____

_____

_____

_____

7

TURNING TRIGGERS INTO
MEDICINE

Now you really get to have a laugh at my expense. I doubled down on the insanity again. What? Yes. Again. Right after Wall Street Collapsed, I got caught up in a financial scam and lost $10,000 of our money. A true criminal scam where I bit the hook, and they took our money in a wire transfer I authorized; I'm sure it went to Nigeria. I'd been scammed because I let myself be scammed. I froze in shame and guilt. Another bad fucking decision, all from my unconscious fears, masked within victimhood.

Looking back, I see this time of "losing" as setting me up to gain self-awareness, self-responsibility, and self-love. But first, I went into fight, then freeze mode and stayed there a few more years. My full understanding of life was contained within the framework of the materialistic Third Dimension—flat, dense, linear, stressful, and all from outside myself. The mystical waking up within would come later. And I would welcome it when I'd had enough of my money-grubbing behaviors and had worn myself out. One of my deaths and rebirths was about money. I had to die to what I thought was important about it by losing everything and being reborn into the understanding that the energy of physical resources, like money and property, were really about a language of appreciation and gratitude and a way to experience the freedom to grow and serve.

Everyone has their version of this pain they seek to numb and hide. For some, this pain is so great they will commit suicide after a major financial scam or failure. That's how tied their ego is to looking good and covering insecurity. Rather than seeing it as an opportunity to learn some of life's big lessons or perhaps even pivoting to help others avoid the same pitfalls, they are willing to die. Me? I had a fucking nervous breakdown with twenty-one years sober!

Sometimes people respond to wealth without growing in generosity. Some people are poor financially and wealthy in other ways. Some have wealth and live in spiritual deprivation, starving to death from a lack of soul-nourishing choices. Some experience the full power of being both wealthy in terms the world recognizes, and also in the realm of spirit. That's the sweet spot for peace: enough money to serve well and enjoy a life lived in love. It's a choice. It's your choice how to play this part of the game of life. When we arrive at this place of self-awareness, we can seek having both a generous financial life and an immeasurable spiritual one, a place of giving and receiving. So, how do we arrive at self-awareness? Through self-observation, *not* observation of others, which is what most of us do.

In the years of processing my shadow, as well as observing the shadow in the collective, I used a method that I created for myself and subsequently in my work.

Shadow work involves bringing unconscious patterns, behaviors, and conditioning to the forefront so we can understand, heal, and integrate them into our lives, bringing greater peace within. Knowing our shadow can bring great joy, magic, personal evolution, and sovereignty.

Over time, when I fully grasped my shadow self, I was able to recognize my trigger, quickly unpack the situation and when I got to the root of my trigger - every part of the trigger was mine, it always is. What do triggers do? They show us where we are not healed. We operate from our deepest unhealed wounds; therefore, when we are triggered by a person, place, or thing, we receive what is happening or being said from that unhealed wound, leaving us often to feel angry, insecure, fearful, jealous, betrayed, sad etc. Think of the trigger as an opportunity of a door opening but often out of fear or our unconsciousness, we slam it shut. What do I mean by that? It's the opening of the process, and if we slam the door shut on the process, we don't allow the opportunity for our growth. The beauty, magic, and joy come from understanding that we are not the victim of the situation, rather, we embrace the trigger as the *medicine* of the teaching.

The trigger is the medicine - either digest it or don't, *and know* that it will continue showing up in your life until you do, or you can remain exactly where you are; how's that working for you?

Our personal responsibility is to look at it, dissect it, and receive the medicine; be grateful for it. The gift of the situation comes when we fully receive and surrender to the medicine. When we do this, we have more clarity and start noticing our troubles are of our own making. The person or the situation that caused the specific trigger is there *for* us; we find gratitude, grace and honor in thanking them for the lessons. Why? They have shown us where we are not free! And that my friends, is a gift.

It's painful to face things head on, but the reward is greater than anything you can imagine. This I can assure you! What's the way out? In! Freedom is found on the other side, coming out from under shame, facing the truth rather than covering it up, and letting go of grandiosity. Scary, I know. I really do.

❧ Write out a current situation in which you find yourself repeatedly triggered?

_____

_____

_____

_____

❧ How are you being triggered? Look solely within; how is that situation triggering you? Is it causing you to feel insecure, angry, resentful, fearful, unsettled, defensive etc.?

_____

_____

_____

_____

❧ Based on your emotions above, where is the situation or person showing you that you have a blind spot? Ex. You allow people to cross your boundaries, or you say, "yes" all the time - which is people pleasing.

_____

_____

_____

❧ Let's dissect the above: you realize people are crossing your boundaries by asking you to do things for them, and you say yes, but you're resentful towards them. The work here is that *you* have to hold your boundaries, because you're not, which is why they keep crossing them.

   ♢ The INside job, is asking yourself, "Why…ex. [do I not hold boundaries]?" (From the example above) Do I feel insignificant? Do I feel if I'm honest they'll judge me? Do I not have any self-value? What is it about yourself that you're experiencing, but you're not looking at?

_____

_____

_____

_____

8

LIVING OUTSIDE IN

Thank God we were in the deep South. Thank God I was so uncomfortable that I had to do something different. I finally got to a point where I had to take on the unsettling vibrations and the suppressing energy I felt. The uncomfortable feeling inside often made it difficult to be in my body, even though I wasn't truly in my body. I didn't understand the world of energy and vibration or how it had been impacting me on multiple levels. The full importance of this awareness would elude me for now, but later it would initiate me into spectacular new experiences. But that would come further down the line.

First, I had to start with something simple. Someone recommended laying on the grass to connect myself to the ground. This is called "grounding." Simple. I started doing this simple thing, often in my business suit. I was the strange and colorful lady in the park on her back on the grass. It helped a little to get me out of my head and put me in touch with an earthy connection. I thought it was so weird.

My emotions needed to be dealt with at a deeper level, yet I had no self-awareness to do so. I was sure that my current troubles couldn't possibly be about me. Clearly, my problems had been created by others, and I was just the clean-up crew.

A friend suggested I seek an energy healer. Listen to your friends; they can spur your growth at just the right time. This kind of "energy work" seemed way too "out there," and "woo-woo," for me; however, I was so uncomfortable in my body, I was willing to do whatever it took. It was only 2005 and the language of energy/frequency and vibration wasn't being used or spoken of; I needed something other than what I was doing, so I gave it a shot.

The healer welcomed me into her home. She brought a high level of sacredness to her work; this was new to me. I was on a massage table, and although she put her hands on me and there were some aspects of what she did that were like a massage, she also lifted her hands off my body and worked in the space around it. It wasn't acupressure, where points on the body like those stimulated by needles in acupuncture were pressed. She was doing something from a higher realm. She moved energy around my body like cars around the racetrack at NASCAR.

I hadn't been really listening to the messages that had been trying to get through to me - from Source, Spirit, God - something higher than me. I didn't have the tools, resources, or knowledge to know or understand that I had not been living authentically from my Soul-Self. I had short-changed myself repeatedly, chasing worldly desires, blaming others, trying anything to validate my fragile sense of self-worth. By choice, I had put myself in a box, created beliefs, conditions and judgements over 21 years that I spent in the fellowship and never allowing for outside information to be a part of my "next level" of training, insight, or awareness. That was my own doing. I not only believed it was the only way to stay sober but believed whole-heartedly, that if you sought more time at your religious or spiritual center that you would eventually drink. I had instilled that fear. A fear so deep that I deprived my need for spiritual growth. My whole world existed within the walls of the fellowship.

I didn't know there are many layers to the human experience that I wasn't privy to, and ultimately shortchanged myself by stunting my own evolution with my limited thinking and beliefs. And it took what it took to get me where I am today. Nothing is a mistake. Ever. Whatever our path is or has been, is exactly where we needed to be at that time, everything serves us in our highest way. Always.

When the energy healer completed her work, she asked if I was open to hearing the visions that came through as she energetically worked on me. Was I open to hearing? Yes. And honestly, it was so far removed from how I lived my life, I couldn't even tell you what she said to me as it pertained to the vibration that I was feeling.

She knew nothing about the details of my life, I had just shown up on her massage table for energy work, and now she sat with me and shared that my dad had been there with us in spirit, sitting next to me. She had seen him attending my healing session with her, sitting with a briefcase on his lap, and when he opened it, butterflies flew out. I burst into tears; she couldn't possibly have known that my dad was dead and that he carried his briefcase with him everywhere like a woman carries a purse. The briefcase was with him constantly, as far back as I could remember. As my dad was recovering in the hospital from neck surgery, at 87, I visited him, and his briefcase was on his belly as he lay in the hospital bed.

Our family had been dysfunctional around communication; expressions of affection were rare. The knowledge that my dad had come through during my healing session gave me a sense of comfort. He'd uttered the words "I love you" two times in my life, but I felt loved by him, and now, I knew he was gone and not gone, and I got it. He was watching over me.

I had known since I was a small child that something was different about me; I could see, feel, and observe the lack of authenticity with adults my entire life. I didn't know what it was or have the capacity to express any of it. I had nowhere to go with all I felt, knew, and could see, so I lost trust and lived in anger and frustration. I squashed my gifts to smithereens, and it took a complete annihilation of my personality, my ego, and an entire collapse of my existence before I would, or could, come into embracing all these amazing gifts and embodying humility.

I am not the only person on the planet who has experienced darkness and a loss of hope—leaving one feeling isolated, lost, unsupported, and confused. But my journey has led me here—sharing my experience, strength, and hope—letting you know you are not alone.

I support clients in opening up to experience the majesty of life. This is done through shadow work; I help them create what's next for them, whatever that may be. It's not a hands-on practice like an energy healer, it's my unique way to swoop in and support a spiritual makeover. Think of what I do as the spiritual version of the series *Queer Eye for The Straight Guy* or *The Nanny*, but with the transformation being one that bridges Spirit and the physical dimension. That's where I've come to after a lot of (painful) training. Until further down the road in my journey, I had lived a typical life in fear of what I didn't know, and pushed my gifts down and aside, not daring to be who I am.

*

Real life, *real life*, was so much bigger than the cycle of working to consume and waiting for time to pass. How much time in your day goes towards watching sports, mindless tv, social media, etc.? Do you realize you are literally watching someone else live out their dreams?

Real life, at the level of Spirit, burns so much more brightly than the ordinary world. Living from the inside out differs greatly from living from the outside in. Are you ready to say yes to higher experiences and a more mystical world view? I believe our society is ready for that light, for that level of consciousness. It's time to change at every level and rethink things we've come to blindly accept when all it takes to change them is to change them, and that is not an easy task. If it were, everyone would simply do it. But we rarely know there's a different way, a different means to the end, another route, or path to take. Instead we hold onto what's no longer working; our outdated beliefs, values, conditions, programming, and that generally get us into more and more uncomfortably, turning into anger and resentment - at others.

What does that look like when our personal transformation moves into the public arena, like writing a book and exposing oneself? For me to lead, guide, and coach, it's necessary to be vulnerable, relatable, trustworthy, and experienced.

I lived my entire life from the outside in, working hard in corporate America, planning for my future and the ability to pay for, and have excellent medical care. It was safe and secure, and I'm grateful for that experience. I had no intention of shifting my path in life out of mainstream, and into the life that exists for me today, even though I was miserable.

Every experience, no matter what it appeared to be or appears to be, is exactly what it needed to be. Twenty-five years in corporate America, specifically in human resources, has given me the opportunities to track human behavior; therefore, I can consult with corporate clients and bridge the gap in many areas that are lacking, ultimately impacting a company's bottom line.

Another shift I am working toward, when I have the opportunity to work with businesses, is bereavement time. Did you know in the U.S. we allow employees only three days of bereavement when someone dies? That doesn't allow for the healing that needs to happen. That doesn't allow a team at work to express compassion for their coworker and offer support that unifies them and brings better collaboration, understanding, and teamwork. That's the time to rally, not bitch. And for the love of God, if a parent dies, a mother - the woman who birthed us - we get three days, *three days,* to grieve before we must get back to work!

Here's another example of what we need to do to burn down the house and rebuild. American businesses expect salaried employees to put in a minimum of fifty-five hours a week, with workloads that often require 80 plus hours to fulfill. Many workers never feel as if the to-do list will go down. It's a trap! Technology has sped everything up and invaded private time with emails and texts. Employers want answers and responses now, even long after we've left the office. Families suffer, marriages suffer, children suffer the inattention of their distracted parents at home. These hours, this self-sacrifice, and the "push-push-push," mentality is energetically and mentally draining. It's soul-killing and ultimately causes illness and disease in the body which you will end up paying for later in life – where is the employer then?

What happens when people who are spiritually alive show up to run a corporation? Water seeks its own level; that's what! What do I mean by this? If I were to isolate this to executive leadership, an A-level executive, in their aptitude and soft skills, will not accept B and C - level executives to work for them; the A-level team will not accept mediocracy. Think of what's possible. I do. And I work to support those soul-feeding leaders and teams, and I am not speaking of woo-woo-ness here, rather helping organizations see the connection of all the dots, on all levels, within the confines of human behavior. Most employees do their craft well, it's the behavior that is generally managed—not the lack of skill.

As I continued this journey of living outside-in while I was struggling to learn how to live from the inside-out, I continued receiving spiritual and energetic smackdowns. A mystical experience would occur rarely, like my dad with his briefcase, and I'd see that as enough to get me through for years, never thinking, feeling, knowing, or believing in my own mysticism.

We have become distracted from caring for our physical and spiritual selves; therefore, we are out of practice being the natural mystics we are underneath ordinary life. Sadly, far too many of us die not knowing life was full of mystical possibilities. Part of my work is to help people wake up from "sleep living." I bet you didn't even realize you were or are, neither did I.

We cannot give away what we do not have; therefore, in order to hold space for others, I had to walk the path myself before I could be of use to anyone else.

Are you ready to say yes to higher experiences and a more mystical world view? It's ok if you're not. Stay open to all possibilities if you can.

  ❦ In assessing your life, are you living from the OUTside - in, or the INside – out?

_____

_____

_____

_____

  ❦ In this chapter, what hit you the hardest between the eyes? Why? Notice how I give you a lot of room to express yourself. Yahoo!

_____

_____

_____

_____

_____

_____

_____

_____

_____

_____

_____

❦ In what ways are you asleep to your true self? Did you notice you were asleep?

_____

_____

_____

_____

❦ If you let your freak-flag fly in terms of how you're living, what could possibly open up in your life?

_____

_____

_____

_____

9

DO NOT RESUSCITATE

No matter where you go, there you are. I had been running and staying busy, but an important aspect of my life, my relationship with Dawson, had died and I was just avoiding the potential harsh reality, and so was she. But based on how we both lived at that time, neither of us would have left our commitment.

By early spring 2007 the stress of all that had transpired was taking its toll on us, and our relationship was unraveling. The South had worn us out like an old pair of shoes that had no tread left. Two of Dawsons siblings, their spouse and kids all lived in Omaha. Her gay brother who we were very close with had just moved back. "Go online and see if there are any good jobs in Omaha," Dawson suggested one day. My discombobulated reactivity to all things Southern and my subconscious sabotaging of just about every situation added to my confusion. I had known Dawson and her siblings since I was 23 years old, and I had my own personal relationship with them. Moving back to California was not a financial option because of our fear. There was only one position in Omaha that fit my experience and background, and it just so happened to fit perfectly. As the Universe would see fit, I landed a great job.

So, we were off for Omaha, Nebraska, and a neighborhood called Dundee, a place known for its one famous resident, Warren Buffett. The homes are a nice size in the area, and Buffett was five doors down from the backside of our American four-square, brick home on 54th Street.

Buffett was known to show up at his neighbors' block parties, eat steak with Bill Gates downtown, and need his 1999 Buick jumped in the parking lot when the battery died. I found it funny that I lived five houses down from one of the wealthiest men on the planet, and my two dogs shat on his lawn. (I picked up after them, but still it was strange and humorous.)

Sadly, my relationship with Dawson had been downgraded by both of us over the past couple of years to more of a business partnership, which left our connection on life support. With the overwhelming stress of all the real-estate issues, our entire connection was spent trying to fix all the outer-world issues, leaving no room to repair the damage to our emotional relationship. We had no intimacy, no love, no caring, no listening—just arguments and power struggles. It was sad to lose the connection to her.

Daily life was stressful, there was still a clusterfuck of real-estate issues to work out. Together, we went through the motions. We fought often; I even lost my shit one day and told Dawson to fuck off. Never in fifteen years had we ever spoken to each other like that, but for some reason, now we did as tempers flared on both sides. It was too much!

While I carried the majority of the financial burden due to having regular income as an employee, the weight of being responsible for the seven mortgages we still had in North Carolina, and our primary residence in Omaha, was a lot. And I no longer felt emotionally supported when I needed it the most. She no doubt experienced me as a drag to be with, and I could understand why. Sadness was always there in the growing space between us. We missed each other even as we shared space and time together.

Once a week, I would pour my heart out to my mother on our regular phone calls, and she took it all in, never giving me unsolicited advice. Mom and I were not close when I was young. I didn't want her teaching me about the birds and the bees, dating boys, sex, or any of it. It wasn't until I got honest and came out to her at thirty-two, that our relationship shifted. She became a true friend, someone who I talked to openly and regularly. She said it was the highlight of her week to share her life with me and hear about mine—even though my life was a shitshow (my description of it, not hers).

In July of 2008, my mom was in hospice care, taken into a deeper grief by losing one of her sisters, my Aunt Eileen, only 25 days earlier. My mom's youngest sister, my Aunt Charlotte, called me a few weeks later, "Your mom isn't doing well. You need to come immediately because she wants to die now, and she's waiting to see you. She won't eat, sit up, or anything; she just wants to depart. She's tired."

I handed things off at work, got myself together, and traveled to be with my mom. Although for days she'd been immobile and listless, it was as if she knew I was coming. When I arrived at her room in hospice, she was sitting up in bed and exclaimed, "What took you so long?" I laughed. "I thought you were sleeping twenty-three hours a day!" She replied, "I was. I've been waiting for you!"

We sat and mourned my Aunt Eileen together. My mother said, "She's younger than me. She wasn't supposed to die first!" These are the stories we tell ourselves that increase our suffering. There really isn't a rule that *the oldest goes first*, but my mother told herself this story, and it made her time in hospice facing her own death even harder. I didn't want to lose my mother, but I knew I needed to support her wishes.

She had a DNR order—Do Not Resuscitate—and my brother Barry and I were prepared to honor her wishes.

We stayed up late and talked and laughed, and she had a burst of energy. She wanted fried chicken and a chocolate shake. I drank her in with my eyes. I held her hand, knowing this was it—the last time for everything. How do you say goodbye to the woman who gave you life? The woman who set the tone for things?

My mom was fun and adventurous, even though she'd been crippled from polio as a child. And she was tough; I had sassed her once while she was baking. She stood in front of me in her flour-spattered apron and grabbed the front of my shirt with one hand and pulled me up out of my chair, backed me up against the wall, and shook her rolling pin in my face. Gritting her teeth, she hissed, "Don't you ever talk back to me like that, young lady!" I never did—again.

As I sat on the edge of her hospital bed and looked her in the eyes, trying to be strong and hold back my emotions, I could feel it coming. A wave thrusting itself up from beneath my feet and crashing into my throat—grief, loss, emptiness.

She looked at me, and I saw bits and pieces of her within me. We put our foreheads together and felt our connection. I thanked her for being a great friend, a good mother, and for teaching me so much about character, integrity, and independence. I thanked her for her humor and for loving me unconditionally my entire life, through all my choices and decisions, and for never judging me for any of them.

Saying goodbye to my mom was one of the most gut-wrenching experiences of my life. Upon my return home, I continued crying for days. I could barely function at work. My mom passed away five days later. I've heard the loss of a parent described as the cutting of an energetic cord from one generation to the next. I felt like a marionette with the strings missing. Functioning was hard, because in this country, we only get three days of bereavement. This was my mom! I needed a year! I would have to mourn her a bit at a time, to live with grief and integrate it into my days and nights, to feel the pain of reaching for the phone to call her, to hold on to memories and let go of her in physical reality.

The grief of losing my mom left me feeling isolated and alone, especially because my relationship with Dawson was dead on its feet. I felt lost without my mother's love and our energetic connection. I could not sustain my trust in people and in life itself. The love I experienced from others always seemed conditional, the same conditional love I gave others. My mom had loved me whole-heartedly, as far as I felt, and I didn't yet seem capable of loving like that. Something would have to shake me loose to learn how to love in the same way, but I was so unaware that I just kept trudging in my usual manner. Little did I know that my aunt's death and my mom's death were the beginning of the biggest shitstorm of my life.

As bad as I felt, I could have used that DNR order myself!

❦ Are you currently hanging onto a job, career, friendship, or marriage that lost its luster long ago? Do you know why you're still hanging on to something that clearly isn't bringing anything to you or for you?
Spill it!

_____

_____

_____

_____

❦ Is there another way to look at the above, possibly seeing it through the lens of liberation versus fear? Oh, yeah, there's fear—otherwise you wouldn't stay in it. Just sayin'.

10

WHAT YOU SEE IN THE MIRROR

I love every life lesson I've had and wouldn't change a thing, but that was not always the case; it was so difficult, challenging, sad, and painful that I would not have wished my journey upon anyone. But after years of doing self-work—creating change, integrating, and transforming—I no longer see my journey from that painful perspective. In fact, it's the opposite. Embracing that I not only walked across the fire, I did handstands across it as well – this was where I learned and know that I am a Warrior of many sorts.

Within thirty days of my mom's passing, I was diagnosed with skin cancer: Basal Cell. And a month later, me and four hundred of my colleagues were laid off from the company a week prior to the collapse of Wall Street in 2008. We were all marched out of the building by security, as if we'd done something wrong. It was the strangest feeling to be a valued and contributing member of the team one day and escorted out of the door the next, holding a little box that represented my life at work and my shoulder bag. I didn't have any sense of completion about my work. I didn't get to say goodbye or hand things over within the department.

My relationship with Dawson was a source of pain and sadness for both of us. And then Wall Street and the economy crashed down around our ears. In the economic downturn, the tenants in our properties lost their jobs and vacated in the middle of the night, leaving the homes vacant for over a year while the world was in a shit storm. Between me being unemployed and no rent coming in from four of those properties for the next 18 months, it was fucking intense! The loan modification game with a total of 8 mortgages from 8 different lenders was mind fuckery at its best, with twenty-one years of sobriety, I had a real-life nervous breakdown.

Dawson and I had been discussing selling our home in Omaha in the spring of 2009. We wanted to be home in Long Beach with our twenty plus year friendships and warmer weather. But when I was laid off in October 2008, it made sense to head there sooner. Three weeks later, we filled a U-Haul and drove back to California, where I thought I had a few good job options lined up. But by the time I got there, the people who had wanted to hire me back had all been laid off, gone out of business, or just plain ran out of work. Things were messy and stressful at best.

After spending a week in Long Beach with me, Dawson returned to Omaha mid-November, and we listed our home —in the dead of winter! In early March 2009, while home alone in Omaha and getting ready to come join me permanently in Long Beach, Dawson had an ovarian cyst erupt. She blacked out from the pain, hit her forehead on a very sharp corner of a doorjamb, and fell back onto the hardwood floor. She came back to consciousness an hour later with our two dogs, Ruby and Oliver, licking the blood off her face. She had cracked her forehead open, down to the bone, from her hairline to her eyebrow. She slid one leg up to get the bottom of her foot on the floor while remaining on her back. With her knowledge of kinesiology, she knew exactly how to maneuver her body to not cause further damage to her neck or possibly paralyze herself. It took her twenty minutes to delicately slide her injured self across the landing at the top of the stairs, about five feet from where she fell on the floor, to get to our bedroom and reach her phone on the nightstand to call for help.

At the hospital, a CT scan revealed her neck was broken, though she wouldn't be paralyzed. This was Dawson's wake up call. She'd reached a crossroads. She was ready to call our relationship dead on arrival. She wanted out. She told me, "I can't wait ten years for you to grow up." I didn't want to hear this. It was hard to look in the mirror and see how right she was. With everything that I was holding and the unbelievable stress of it all, I pretty much stayed embodied in anger, living out the stories over and over, gasping for air, and yet I was relieved from the burden of my relationship.

Dawson called me out about the reality that we'd been deeply disconnected for a long time. She didn't see the potential to repair our relationship. She was right. I hated that she was right. Dawson and I had a soul contract that had come to its completion, and I knew that. This was a moment of my claircognizance. While I knew it was a "contract," I was still years away from even knowing what this meant. But the seed was soon planted.

Could I have imagined my life would be where it was? Hell no. My mom's death, my partner of seventeen years gone, my aunt's death, lost friendships, my career stalled, my self-worth at a low, my income gone, my security gone, the calamity of Wall Street, financial losses on property, and the skin cancer, with all this coming at me, and having a nervous breakdown, it still never occurred to me that alcohol would fix any of it. And it wouldn't be able to numb the already numb.

If I had chosen to drink, I would be dead or in prison. Maybe, given my tendency to overdo things, I would have been dead *in* prison. I have been sober for over thirty-five years, and I will never drink again, not even on my death-bed. My life circumstances, as bad as they were, were not setting me up to drink; this thought never even came to me. While my stubbornness was often a great champion to self-motivation, I had that sense of knowing again. The sense, a feeling, a knowing that something big was happening, and it was about to get really fucking hot in this fire that was rolling up on me in the form of a death and rebirth. I was about to burn, to blow the ashes into the wind. I didn't know it, but Spirit was setting me up for some deeply profound spiritual work. I was lighting the match to **Burning Down the House.**

*

When we seek our Soul's path, the reason for our existence here, each person discovers a unique reason—as unique as their fingerprints. Each soul is on its own journey.

But first I had to do the pre-requisites; I was learning I had been attached to people, places, and things. I needed to stop holding on as if my life depended on it. I needed not to be needy—emotionally. I started asking what was bringing me joy. At this time, nothing was, so I had to change my perception and change how I was treating myself.

I took a long look in the mirror and realized I did not know who the fuck I was at forty-seven, now that all my labels were missing - torn off like an overused, unwelcomed bandage.

I learned that some things naturally ended and holding that reality with grace and gratitude would allow the cleansing fire of loss to set me free. With that freedom, I would rise from the ashes as a more mature and loving version of myself. We get what we need to grow in Divine love, Divine work, and Divine timing—not necessarily what we want! This can only occur when we let go of control and start to trust and have faith that it's all working out *for* us and not happening *to* us. But often, in our limited ways, we think we know better so we continue trying to control it all.

For a time, we may miss opportunities to see or know our teachings. Our self-awareness can be clouded by fear, ego, and unhealed stuff. We can miss those moments of clarity that help guide us forward. And when we miss them, they will come around again and again and again until we *get it*. And when we don't, they will get more and more painful until we see them, and they receive our attention.

I had to experience what is called an ego death, also known as The Dark Night of the Soul (DNOTS). I had to learn to surrender to what is every time I tried to control my circumstances; otherwise, it was just another painful spiral down. Through my journey and over time, I've learned to surrender much more quickly, but not after several attempts at digging my heels in repeatedly, trying to control the chaos of my outer world, which is ultimately the reflection of my inner world.

I would die to my old self repeatedly; I would re-define myself after each rebirth, taking more care of my relation to Spirit, to Source. So far to go and so little time. Just the right challenge.

❦ What if everything you're experiencing is perfect—the perfect alignment for your growth and expansion? All of it happens *for* you, can you reframe and observe your story from a different place?

_____

_____

_____

_____

❦ Each soul is on its own journey – are you following your own unique blueprint? Or are you in the "herd" mentality?

❦ What labels do you identify with in your life? Parent, career, what you own, what you drive...If you sat in reflection, who are you without your outside labels? Scary thought! I know.

_____

_____

_____

_____

❦ Where in your life are you emotionally attached to people, places and things? How is this serving you in which you are not able to find it from within?

_____

_____

_____

_____

❦ How willing are you to surrender your ego to embrace yourself? NOTE: this is not a onetime calling – to surrender.

_____

_____

_____

_____

11

MY CALLING IS YELLING

By early spring 2009, I was burdened with life; the complete collapse of my entire existence all at once caused anxiety and depression, and I was over the edge. I wanted answers as to why my life had blown apart and into tiny little shrapnel. I was having a real-life nervous breakdown with twenty-one years sober. *WTF? What did I do to deserve all this?* I kept asking myself and the Universe repeatedly.

One morning, I was in a complete emotional meltdown, a deep well of so much pain and heartache. In the fellowship of AA, we're trained to work with another alcoholic when we're in this kind of pain, to find grace, gratitude, and to serve ourselves by serving others, and most of the time, this effort worked. But not this morning.

I was in complete annihilation of self, sobbing and yelling repeatedly in the second person, "You will not work with another alcoholic or attend another meeting!" It was such an odd thing to come flying out of my mouth, considering I was going to ten meetings a week while unemployed. I was committed to and dedicated to the program, to my recovery, and fellowship for two decades, but here I was telling myself that *I needed to sit in my pain and feel every throbbing cell in my body.* I was exhausted.

Another cathartic experience arose later that night as I was standing at the kitchen sink in an emotional upheaval and a breakdown of self, crying so hard I could barely take in any air. Suddenly, I heard a voice in my head, *Child, if you can hang on through all this pain and sadness, the gifts that you'll receive will be equal to or greater than the pain you are in.* It was so clear; I heard the angels—so I thought. While I was in emotional despair for the next eighteen months, I hung onto the words I had heard so clearly. I still could not comprehend what was happening, neither could anyone else, including my AA sponsor and my doctor. I felt as though my body was tiny little molecules outside myself, that I was not in my body or my right mind. The anxiety often overwhelmed my sense of trust in others, and most definitely trust in myself.

A fucking disastrous hot mess—that's what I represented in that moment—feeling self-destructive, lost, and abandoned. I was looking for crazy ways to get out of the pain I was in. I didn't know that my experience was all about growth and change. I share this so you'll embrace yourself through your darkest times and begin to open to *why.* It's all loveable. It's all understandable. It's all OK. It's all part of being human. Life is fucking hard—by design.

*

I can drive anything: boats, limos, fifth-wheels, motorcycles, tractors, dump trucks, cars, pickup trucks, etc. I always drove in the number one lane, otherwise known as the in the fast lane, when I drove on the 405 freeway in Los Angeles, with seven lanes in each direction. But let me tell you, amid the stresses in my life, and all the anxiety I was experiencing, I would barely get into the fast lane when I'd think, *Oh my god, I am in over my head!* And would move five or six lanes while wondering, *What would happen if I just drove my car into the center divider?* And other moments of pondering, *What if I just swerve, right now, and drive my car into on-coming traffic?* But I couldn't bear the thought of hurting someone else. *Maybe I could drive my car off the end of a pier into deep water.* But I didn't really want to annihilate myself. I wanted it all to just fucking go away! All the problems. It was a giant loop of big ass problems going round and round like the world's largest Farris wheel. I got to the point where several times I considered committing armed robbery so that I could go to prison and not have to deal with my life any longer. I considered that a very real option.

To go from a seemingly perfect life to the shitshow I was in was not something I, or anyone around me, could understand. I stood there raw and exposed, with nowhere else to hide. It was as if the curtain from the great Oz was revealed. My worst behaviors were coming to the surface, and I tried to cover them up as quickly as possible through my irrational justifications.

It was so intense, so painful, and I was so full of sadness and fear of so much uncertainty that the cells in my body were vibrating. I was being stripped of all of who I was then, only I didn't understand this in the slightest. I had zero connection to myself, my Essence, my Soul, and had no awareness around self-awareness. If I just kept pointing out your faults, and yours, yours too, it was a great distraction from looking at my own shortcomings.

*

I was open to new things and even said yes to the opportunity to dance with a five-foot boa constrictor and a five-foot python, each snake laid separately across the back of my neck with my arms straight out to a T. While there was tremendous fear around the experience, I did it anyway, and the dance with the snakes released fears I had about aspects of Mother Nature. I learned how to move free of fear and trepidation.

I did yoga regularly, tried to calm my monkey mind and meditate, was more active with friends, attended workshops about spirituality, and threw myself into learning new practices, and I turned to my trusted, battle-tested friend, the medium.

I felt the pull to attend the biggest yoga festival in the United States, Bhakti Fest. Bhakti means devotion. I didn't know what it would be like, but I kept seeing signs, literal flyers for it everywhere, in the most uncommon places, and I had enough awareness to see the pattern in this. I allowed my intuition to lead the way. I jumped in to see for myself and registered for this first ever Bhakti Fest in the United States in September 2009. I mustered the courage to go to something this big for five days and nights, all by myself. I was seeking something in my life, anything other than the shitty place I was in, which lacked fun, joy, and gratitude.

I borrowed a tent and sleeping bag from a friend and went off to Joshua Tree, California, by myself, but also in the company of a couple thousand people. It was five days and nights of celebration, connection, music, and yoga. It was a family-friendly gathering with children's activities and a safe environment to play and dance and sing. No alcohol was allowed on site. Workshops provided a taste of devotional singing and breath work. Special events exposed me to a variety of teachers who shared their experiences and practices, and that taste pointed me toward my next steps on the journey. There were two stages with sacred chant music, ranging from traditional music from around the world to devotional rock and roll in Sanskrit. Bhakti fest went from early morning to very late at night. There was clean food and a direct connection to the desert and the beautiful illumination of the night sky.

I walked around barefoot, feeling the hot powdery soil beneath my feet, taking in the smells of incense. The warm breeze blended the delicious scents of sage, ocotillo, and palo santo, sending my nose and body into a peaceful and grounding place. The cornucopia of smells lingering in the air from food trucks; Indian spices, vegetarian, Greek, vegan, pizza, and the delicious faint metallic taste in the air blowing in from the nearby rock formations. There were colorful tents and works of art and healers of all kinds. It was all about sacred devotion. I could be in the middle of the celebration joyfully dancing, feeling connected to an exuberant community, or choose to walk peacefully alone around the parameter of the property at night enjoying the stars and listening to the bubbling water fountains, soft conversations, laughter, and the faint sound of music in the distance drifting toward me. One day and night rolled into the next; it was heaven on earth.

The amount of love and community I discovered at Bhakti Fest was beyond anything I'd ever experienced. It felt different from any other big group event I had attended. There was a different air to it all, people connected, they didn't just talk. They were soft in their essence, present with you, interested in giving and receiving, connected, and connecting to Source. You could leave your purse on the vast rug in front of the stage and go off to dance for hours and come back to find it untouched. I sat under a sunshade talking to people from all over the country from a variety of backgrounds, and we all had one thing in common that I quickly noticed; we all aspired to live from the *heart*—a place so unfamiliar to me it would take several years of rough and tumble before I dropped from my head and into my heart.

Teachers and healers of many sorts say, "Get out of your head and into your heart," but they never tell you how to do so. You can't just go, "Ok! I'm in my heart." I wish! In my personal discovery, the way into the heart is through shadow work.

It can be very hard to make changes when you're only around those with whom you have history and who persist in seeing you as you were. It was lonely when I no longer resonated with the very foundation I once built an entire life on.

I had yet to discover my new path, my new community, family, tribe. I wandered aimlessly for many years but because I took action to step out of my comfort zone, I discovered new tribes and new friends who met me where I was *now*. I added exciting new people to a few of my favorite old friends and kept the momentum of my growth heading in the right direction. This combination gave me roots and wings.

*

During a full on life collapse, I was not capable of understanding that I was on a spiritual quest of some sort, and with so many crises encapsulating me, all I could see, feel, and think was I somehow needed to put this shit back together—a job, a relationship, money, my retirement portfolio, new friends—not realizing I was putting it together from the outside, *again*.

I was building my spiritual muscles as a student. I was fighting for a different way to live than the miserable fucking place I was in, but I did not know how I was going to maneuver my way out of this fight—with myself. I was so emotionally bloodied, but I learned what I was made of: guts, grit, will, strength, courage, heart, compassion, and the bravery to move forward. I was fighting for my life. To walk through that kind of fire—fanning my own fucking flames, often lost, confused, depressed, and all the while empty on the inside with zero family to support any of it—fuck, it was hard. I won't lie. The beauty is that so many amazing things have transpired since those days that it almost doesn't feel as if it ever even happened.

*

Being a fighter saved my life as a baby who was described as a "blue baby." I was told that during my birth, I was heading out feet first and blue. The doctor shoved me back inside, opened my mom up, and unwrapped the umbilical cord from around my neck. But the doctor didn't believe I would live. Within a few hours, I had turned myself around. My mom gave birth to me, and I was blue gray at first, but I kicked and struggled, and my skin went from white to pink to orange to screaming red. I hollered. I flailed. I breathed. I was strong. My mom told me that story when I was thirty-five years of age. She said that she knew I could endure any struggle, any obstacle in life, that my will to live was so apparent to her on that day of my birth. I cried for a week, finally understanding that inherent fight in me. That fight, both an asset and a liability in extremes eventually came into balance. Is there something in your life you've always wanted to do, but the fear of doing it alone has held you back?

❦ Is your Calling whispering, yelling, tapping you gently on the shoulder calling to you?

❦ Are you listening? Perhaps you don't know you're supposed to be listening. What would happen if you listened?

Let's pause for a moment…
Listening simply means *paying attention*.

❧ Where are you fighting, digging in, resisting, and causing yourself emotional harm by blaming others? Nothing will ever feel better for you until you look within first.

_____

_____

_____

_____

_____

❧ Is it possible that these crises, situations, and circumstances are happening for you and not to you? See prior chapter questions on the Teaching, the Medicine, and the Gift set in motion by triggers.

_____

_____

_____

_____

_____

_____

_____

_____

_____

_____

_____

_____

_____

12

GIFTS

As a small child, I had always sensed that we lived more than one lifetime, that our soul continued to come back over and over, though I did not understand the purpose of this at such a young age. I also didn't understand why or how I knew this. Nothing in my secular family in middle-American culture, in the 1960s, with limited access to knowledge and no books about the subject, had seeded these ideas. However, I can remember the knowingness starting around the age of six. So how did I know about reincarnation? Because this life wasn't my first rodeo. That's why!

It wasn't even when my life blew apart that I understood the deeper meaning of my existence. It also wasn't cancer. Situations kept going awry in my life to get me on a path to consciousness, and each time I denied the path, it became more and more painful until I fully surrendered to the teaching, to that layer of my onion and releasing control, seeing my victim mentality, and keeping myself open to all things. My life became surrounded by others who showed me the way to another path, a path of consciousness.

All my trials and tribulations offered me so much experience, and these experiences brought me to remembering who I am—my Soul's journey, not my personality's journey. I gained a deeper understanding of this later when my mystical gifts were shown to me, when I started gathering up all the parts of myself that remembered, knew, or felt the wisdom within.

If God resides *in* us, in our temple body, why then do we spend so much time residing, gathering, and living in materialistic things that live *outside* of our bodies versus nurturing god within us and taking care of what matters the most? Food for thought.

The Soul's path made sense to me, and when that seed was planted for me, I stayed open to the idea, to the possibility. The more I experienced, the more the soul's path came into view, into remembrance, and it certainly explained a lot and connected so many dots in my life.

At a young age, I felt an innate, ancient wisdom within my body, which I never spoke of, to anyone, ever. I'd always felt pulled toward Egypt. I stopped talking about this desire as a teenager, when my family or friends seemed to doubt me or make fun of me. "Why Egypt?" they'd ask. All I could do was shrug my shoulders and respond quietly, "I don't know. But I'm going back to Egypt for sure." Back to? I'd never been. But I knew I had. Whether that made sense to others, it made complete sense to me. I'd buried this dream as deep as a pharaoh's tomb. This sense of "knowing" was in my body at a visceral level.

As an adult, I could manage, with zero experience or training, the logistics of very large and complex projects. I was and am a great recruiter and leader in developing talent. In a decade, I have hired and relocated hundreds of individuals in the companies for whom they wanted to work. When given a problem, I would find the solution quickly, eliminating the additional steps my peers and often my superiors thought was necessary. I would connect all the dots and thread the entire situation together for them to illustrate the bigger picture and get to the solution quickly and efficiently. I didn't understand my innate sense or understanding until I learned, two decades later, in a shamanic medicine journey, that I had been a General in several past lifetimes.

While the experience of this military-planning sensibility might seem far-fetched to some, it made perfect sense to me. In fact, learning this detail about myself had also been a great relief. I finally understood that I could trust my inner knowing about certain things. My logistical and strategic mind serves me well as a guide, a way-shower and it serves others well too. And I don't suppress it. I work to amplify this natural ability. It's what supports the family system, the individual, and even the CEO in having their breakthroughs. It's why I can advise people who are well known and keep their confidences and honor their privacy without being enamored by the glamour—because I'm focused on supporting their evolution and the essence of who they are, in the same manner I would a hardened prisoner; I'd be focused on supporting their evolution and the essence of who they are, as well.

When breast cancer showed up four years after the basal cell, I was honed by the fire again, but my emotional maturity was still holding me back. I'd have to face that fully. I'll tell you more about that next.

But first, let's look at your calling, your distant past, your path, this lifetime, and the way you are being forged in the fire.

❧ Where do you believe, think, or feel gifts come from?

_____

_____

_____

_____

❦ Do gifts and their origins differ from talents or skills? What I believe is that gifts come through from past lives; mine did, anyway. Please also note that gifts are referenced in this book as part of the trigger-medicine-gift process and differ from these gifts.

❦ If you were coming to the end of your life, what could you do differently now in order to fulfill your purpose? If you've not thought about this, perhaps it would be a good time to do so.

_____

_____

_____

_____

Take some time to ponder this next question.

❦ What do you inherently know or do that came with you into this lifetime.

_____

_____

_____

_____

This is a gift!
Keep this awareness of how the deep past and your present are dancing together.

13

THE FUEL FOR FULL POWER

To this day, I don't know what propelled me, and yet I do, to make an appointment for a mammogram. I had avoided them for nine years; I did not want the radiation and there wasn't a history of cancer in my family, but suddenly, I felt inspired to schedule it. I expected a call back with the news that all was well, but I got a call back for a biopsy, and I still thought nothing of it. But there's a sound you never forget in the voice of a doctor when they request you get off the plane immediately and call them back on their cell phone.

I never thought I would have breast cancer, I felt like I'd done my dance with cancer and that there was a one-cancer maximum per lifetime. Nope. I thought I'd learned all there was to learn from cancer. Nope. It turns out I needed breast cancer to find my full power.

I had just boarded the plane, had my carry-on loaded in the overhead bin and was settling into my seat, about to power down my phone, when my doctor called. She heard the background noise in the cabin. "Where are you?" She asked.

"I just boarded my plane in Orange County, heading to Dallas and on to Arkansas."

"Where are your support group, family, and close friends— Arkansas or California?" She asked.

"My closest people are here in California." I responded.

"Get off the plane and call me right back. It's not good, Cheryl!"

The news went in my ear, but something inside went numb and couldn't process it. I dissolved in quiet tears and a flight attendant thoughtfully helped me gather my luggage to deboard. The people around me could tell I'd received bad news. As I was leaving the plane, several passengers extended their kindness: "I'll pray for you," "I hope everything turns out," "God Bless." It was sweet to receive compassion from total strangers. It taught me something important about trusting the world, and even though I was in disbelief about my dire medical situation, I took in the kindness that was coming toward me.

I was guided off the plane by a flight attendant. She put her arm around me, and up the gangway we went until we reached the gate. There, my body went limp, and I slid down the wall to the floor, weeping.

I called my friend Todd, so choked up I could barely speak. He picked me up, and we headed to his house in Laguna Beach. Todd called my friend Maya, who, upon hearing the news, left work and drove from San Diego. Then he called my dear friend Phyllis, and she rushed over. My brother Barry came from Oregon to stay for a week close by to support me. Earlier in my life, I wasn't good at receiving. Now, I had no choice. I would have to receive to make it through the real hard shit. It was a great teaching.

I had another difficult call to make to my Aunt Charlotte, who is very dear to me. She had been like a mother to me since my mom died; she was the last living relative on my mom's side of the family. When I told her about my biopsy and diagnosis, she cried. I assured her I would get through it, that this was just another bump in the road, or a lump in the breast—a malignant one.

Stage 3C. It sounds innocuous enough, just a number and a letter, like the cup size of a bra. Barry's girlfriend at the time, Brenda, had recently gone through breast cancer, so he'd become well-versed in the language of chemo, radiation, mastectomy, and reconstruction. He had me ask my doctor a lot of questions that I would not have known to ask. I did not know what would come next, but I had people who cared about me. I trusted them and relied on them. They had my back. They also had my front.

Even as I experienced a new level of life crisis, I was recognizing some of the spiritual medicine. Medicine, in the spiritual sense, represents taking in the teaching. In this case, my medicine was seeing how I needed to learn to receive help and support and let go of being so independent and doing it all myself. This was a big shift for me and my ability to experience gratitude in the middle of the shit storm.

My first six chemo treatments were scheduled three weeks apart, and I was constantly in travel mode to pull it all off with the job I was so grateful to have because it made my financial life and medical needs work for my situation. My southern client was kind, bosses in all levels of management and co-workers collaborated with me tirelessly, and every time I went back on-site between treatments, I was met with, "If there's anything you need, please ask!"

Until that time, the divide between "well" people and "ill" people seemed like a protective barrier that had me on one side of that line. Now I know the truth; we're all one test and one phone call away from the news that puts us on the other side of that line, having experiences that can break or make us.

From breast cancer, I learned big experiences can be integrated by the personal choice to learn from everything and be grateful for all of it—and I mean all of it. Gratitude helps us rise like the phoenix from the flames, and sometimes it takes us a while to get there. Anger holds an energetic frequency that doesn't allow the body to heal and where gratitude does. For those of you who haven't experienced cancer, it takes time and layers of healing to find a morsel of gratitude. So please try not to direct someone from a place you've never stood. And just because someone looks healthy, doesn't mean they aren't in grief and sadness with the physical repercussions from treatment and surgeries that often come with it. Radiation. Chemo. Anesthesia. Lymphatic system. Slicing and dicing the body. it's a lot.

This hard shit is a *process,* and there are no shortcuts, no ways to bypass the fire, and it certainly doesn't help to smear a thin layer of toxic positivity or spiritual bypassing over the top. This is big stuff, and it needs to be handled with care and compassion. These are the times when it's great to have an experienced person in the mix to help get everyone through the shitstorm. How can someone lead others out of a battle they've never fought?

Facing what scares us in our darkest hours, days, months, years, and sharing it in a safe community requires a special courage, a courage I have come to know well and can lead and guide individuals and teams of people out of the storm. I had cancer as yet another teacher; there are many types, and ways of teachings in life. You'll find them in your life, and the payoffs will amaze you.

❦ If finding lessons in your journey has a payoff, have you found yours? If so, where?

_____

_____

_____

_____

❧ In the middle of a storm, crisis, illness, etc., can you find gratitude?

❧ Is it easier for you to receive care than give it? Or is it easier for you to give care than to receive it?

❧ What would a balance between receiving and giving look like in your life?

_____

_____

_____

_____

❧ Do you have a good support group of close family and good friends to *hold space* (meaning to support without input, judgment, forcing opinions, etc.) for you during the process you're in?

_____

_____

_____

_____

☙ If not, why not? How much energy are you putting into a relationship that isn't nurturing you? Or, if you're always being criticized or judged in this relationship, why do you choose to stay? Have you grown past some of these connections?

_____

_____

_____

_____

☙ Are you open to creating space in your life for new ones?

_____

_____

_____

_____

14

LEARNING THROUGH DISEASE

J ust four months before my diagnosis, I met Krisi online. She lived in Nashville, and I had my consulting gig working in Arkansas. I spent time in California once a month for an extended weekend. We connected romantically and would meet in Memphis for a weekend, or I would fly out of the small regional airport in El Dorado on a nine-seater commuter plane into Nashville on a Friday afternoon and return late Sunday night. When I went to California for long weekends, I would fly Krisi out to be with me in Laguna Beach or Long Beach. We loved our time together.

Krisi was soft spoken, intelligent, caring, and kind, with the most beautiful energy. I learned so much from our relationship, and she said she did too, as hard as it was. Our connection was still very new when I received the diagnosis, and she chose to go deeper with me to see what could come of it. And I made the choice to let someone who I didn't know well, see me be truly vulnerable.

Even though the complications of cancer made it a stressful time, we still had a lot of fun. But I was in no position to be able to show up emotionally for someone else. It just wasn't happening no matter how much effort I gave it. I didn't have the capacity.

She had a seven-year-old son named Eli; he was smarter than both of us combined, which made it a blast to play games with him. He happily destroyed us in some games, but when we played Monopoly, he wasn't out to make a killing in real estate and even loaned me Monopoly money at no interest when I ran out!

My parents supported my brothers and me, but they didn't provide the comfort, nurturing, and communication I saw flow so effortlessly between Krisi and Eli. Eli clearly knew he was loved and didn't think he had to earn it. He was fully self-expressed. He didn't have to prove anything. Eli shared his thoughts and emotions with his mom easily, and he knew how to listen to others and respond to their feelings.

Cocaine and alcohol had been my way of numbing my feelings. Why did they need to be numbed? Because I didn't know how to process them, who to share them with, or how to communicate with any level of emotional intelligence and spiritual depth. Everything authentic about me was buried under layers of unprocessed emotion. I'd made decisions that added to that wall of separation between me and the people I loved over the years. I thought it was self-protection, it wasn't, I was dying behind that wall.

Eli had positive attention whenever he needed it; he had compassion and the capacity to be at peace with himself. When I was young, I acted out to get attention by stealing from the local liquor store, stealing dollar bills from my parents, and getting into trouble in school by clowning around constantly. *Look at me! I'm the kid out on the edge!* Why had I chosen that way of being? Because my deepest fear was that there was something wrong with me that made me unworthy of love. I didn't know then that it wasn't me. It was what my parents were given, and it was even less love, nurturing, and compassion that they received, and up the food chain it goes, to all to the ancestors before them.

I had pretended to have it together, marching around looking confident, when in truth, I hid that I didn't think I was enough. What if I was honest about that? And what if I learned to love myself first, care for myself properly, so I could trust love and support when it flowed to me from others?

Krisi read to Eli every night until he fell asleep, a little contented smile on his lips. She walked him to school and back. They talked about their interior lives and their feelings. She guided him through tough times, and together, they talked about what was possible for his future. It was feasible to be vulnerable *and* powerful in combination. I had mistakenly believed vulnerability was weakness and powerlessness. I soaked up what I was learning from them like a student in the front row.

Krisi was a good partner and had a beautiful spirit. She dove into reading about my cancer and asking sophisticated health questions, as I was too tired and overwhelmed to track. It was hard enough for me to just get through the physical demands of the experience of breast cancer. We loved each other, and together, we limped through.

I had a port placed in the upper part of my left breast/ chest area. The chemo went in. My hair fell out. The first handful of hair dropped as I sat in my car, sizing myself up in the rear-view mirror, I asked myself, *Are you going to give your power over to this?* Fuck no! I called my hair stylist, and she got excited, "Come right now. I'll squeeze you in!" She shaved my head.

Everyone must have heard us laughing and me crying because when she was done, everyone in the salon clapped. In that moment, I knew I had taken back my power. I was looking cancer square in the eyes. Addiction wasn't an issue; I wasn't even tempted to numb myself to escape the reality I was living. I was stone-cold sober; the thought of drinking or drugging was not even entertained by me, not once.

Chemo required my warrior spirit to rise to the challenge. After my first treatment, I didn't sleep or eat for four nights and five days. My bones were ice cold. I had high anxiety, and the worst constipation ever; it felt like giving birth.

After thirty-two years clean and sober, I made a conscious decision to use cannabis to support my recovery process each time I had chemo. This differed greatly from what I'd done in my youth using alcohol and the dark energy of destructive drugs that came with partying to try to find connection to others. I used cannabis in a disciplined way and as part of a regimen of self-care. I used it with respect and self-honor and felt moved to stop using cannabis when the cancer treatment was completed.

I was deeply grateful to the spirit of the plant and what it made available to me. I learned an important lesson about medication, medicine, and healing of body and soul. It was a gift of sovereignty; I was making decisions from my truth, my authenticity, and doing what was right for me at the right time. Breast cancer taught me to respect my Divine intuition rather than rely solely on someone else's judgements, opinions, or criticism.

*

I was so tired for so long I became depressed, and realized years later, this was when I entered the Dark Night of the Soul. I lost days and weeks to feeling morose. I was sick and miserable. Some days, my accomplishments were limited to using the remote, and wiping my ass.

I had been living in a corporate apartment in Arkansas, that was provided by my client, while consulting on a massive project. I would fly home to California every three weeks for my chemo treatment. I was so physically depleted after the first treatment that my childhood friend Caryn flew back with me, as I wouldn't have been able to deal with airports on my own. I was brought in by wheelchair, pre-boarded, and wheeled again to the next gate. I had no energy to hold up my body as I slumped sideways into the wheelchair.

My body felt like that of someone who was 110 years old—frail, brittle, stiff, and fragile. When I had enough strength to get out of bed, I shuffled and held onto countertops and leaned on walls for support. My bones were so cold, I didn't even feel like a warm-blooded mammal. Feeling a tenuous hold on life, I felt the closeness of death, and facing it opened gratitude for my life.

Seeing others who were even more fragile than me going through the physical effects of chemo gave me empathy and compassion in a way I had never felt before. And for the time we spent together, Krisi hung on with me, learning as I learned, growing as I grew, and learning to love through difficulty in the messiness of it all.

Cancer taught me more about what it is to be a spiritual being living in a physical body. I would eventually come to love the battle scars and the shifts in how I looked. It was traumatic. My breasts had been a fun part of being a woman. They were an important part of lovemaking. I enjoyed how I looked and how I felt with two healthy breasts. The process of letting go of a body part was difficult for me emotionally. I cried over it for ten years, and I gave myself permission to do so. I have done an enormous amount of healing around it. Healing the trauma comes in layers.

There were sad moments preparing for the mastectomy. It was hard to come to terms with having my breast cut off, and I turned and twisted every way imaginable to get the situation to work differently. But surrendering and accepting reality takes love-warrior energy; it takes courage to see what's actually there and not what we wish it could be.

After a month of grieving, I was emotionally ready to let go of my right breast. I was fully in for having a mastectomy. Krisi and I did a sweet ceremony for the releasing of my breast the night before the surgery. Mastectomy and removal of eleven lymph nodes under my right armpit. Done. Chemo. Done. Terrible third-degree burns to the skin from radiation. Wow. Didn't see that coming. That set me up for a limited option for breast reconstruction. That was a shit show with a total of ten surgeries because of the complexity and complication I experienced.

When I look at my body and all its scars, I'm grateful, and I didn't always feel that way. It took so many teachings and so much self-awareness to come into. My body looks like a fucking battleground, and it took a minute for me to accept and honor my scars from this fiasco. I was able to move myself out of that mental and emotional space rather quickly and embody my battle wounds by standing in front of a mirror in my birthday suit, flex my muscles, and say, "Fuck yeah! I'm a warrior." And not only do I have one hell-of-a story but also the fucking scars to remind me of where I have been and where I am now. Today, I look myself in the mirror with a smile and say thank You for all you've gotten us through – often.

During all my travels, I stuck out like a bald cancer patient. Oh wait, I am bald. Oh, and I have cancer! I had amazing conversations—in airports, restaurants, on the street, in shops, yoga class, you name it. I remember thinking, *Would it be so hard for people to just be this open and kind all the time?* Just because we can't see someone's illness, pain, suffering, trauma, or sadness, doesn't mean it isn't going on right under the surface. Why not assume a loving stance in the world?

The gifts of cancer were becoming clearer in more situations. I was a deeper, more caring, more courageous person.

And because I was transparent, things opened up for others as well. During my consulting gig in Arkansas, I worked with a man named Larry, who took his fifteen-minute breaks daily when I worked through mine. And what did I do? I judged him for it, which was so fucking arrogant on my part, but a big teaching was about to show up. We had over seven hundred employees in the corporate office, and who came to me one day? Larry does; that's who. In his very thick, slow, southern drawl, he said, "Ms. Cheryl, I know you've been going through cancer this past year. I was just diagnosed with a rare and deadly cancer, and I'm very scared."

His eyes welled with tears, trying not to show the depth of his fear and sadness. I listened to him share his experience and expressed my emotions in response as tears rolled down my face. I sat with Larry for a solid hour as we talked about treatment, nutrition, spiritual growth, family, community support, and how mental strength and will are important—no matter how bad we feel physically.

That was a powerful lesson for me that day and one I don't think I'll ever forget. The person whom I secretly sat in contempt and judgement over was the one person who needed me the most. I could also give him so much compassion, kindness, and support, and he had also shown me who I had become. It was bittersweet.

Through breast cancer, I dropped a lot of self-focus, judgmental thoughts, limiting beliefs, pride, being the victim, and a lot of other nonsense. Those things still show up in me because they do for everyone. We can't help it. I currently let those distractions visit briefly, but I don't let them move into my psyche or my heart and stay there. I know how to process—quickly—and get to the place where I'm clear in my intention and genuinely useful to others.

*

I kept seeing an advertisement for a special weekend for cancer patients called Camp Bluebird. I knew deep down that I needed to be there, even though I didn't know what it was, but I was at the beginning stages of that doomsday feeling I had in 2008—that I was going over the edge. I needed to connect with those who could relate to where I was and what I was going through. I needed help from those in my cancer tribe.

At camp, I met friends who, under other circumstances, I probably would have never connected with. We were from different worlds, but we met up in cancer world and bonded instantly based on our triumphs, fears, scars, and stories.

Nursing students from the local university are required as part of their curriculum to volunteer at Camp Bluebird, and because they love it, many choose to return for years. The nurses said they always get more from the experience than they give, they knew how to love and serve. I was learning to do that as well. It was fun at camp. There were events, group conversations, lots of play, and there was entertainment. It was the cheesiest, most hilarious, and absolute most fun I had had in a long time.

I also ended up being a gay ambassador because most of the patients at camp came from conservative Christian congregations and were convinced, they "didn't know any gay people." One thing I've learned – I can't expect others to know what they don't know, therefore as a gay woman, it is my opportunity to share what gay people go through versus the straight people trying to guess. So, I let them know it was safe to ask me literally anything they felt comfortable asking. I shared openly and honestly what it was like living in a straight-dominated world, what it was like for someone who realizes they are gay when the families and culture around them reject the essence of their soul, and the shame some people in some places want to project onto it. I demystified the mystified for my new friends. They shared with me that I had opened their eyes and minds.

Coming out to my family took me ten years, not because of my fear of how they would react, but because I needed to be in my own acceptance and self-love, and that took a while. When I finally came out to my mom, she sent me a letter *thanking me* for giving her the opportunity to dive into her judgments, blind spots, and misguided beliefs. My truth set me free and opened a door to a deeper relationship with my mom.

Life in the closet is painful in ways understood best by those who've been in the closet. The phrase "in the closet" usually relates to gay people. But there's a way of being in the closet that means hiding out and not sharing the truth about yourself in a variety of ways. Being locked up in a closet is not a good place to be when there's a big world out there. At Camp Bluebird, while fighting cancer, I lived my full, authentic truth, which I hope inspired others to live theirs, whatever it might be.

If you haven't had a major illness, I hope you can pick up some of the teachings without having to get cancer or any other illness. Our physical body is the last house on the block (with the exception of hereditary diseases or extreme external environments) when we don't deal with our emotions, stress, trauma, or pain, it shows up as illness or disease. Sorry for the news flash.

*

When I look into my eyes in the mirror, I see reflected all the spiritual healers and wisdom teachers who helped me live. They shared their knowledge and skills so generously with me. It took support from many of them for many years for me to stand where I do now, with a great deal of physical, emotional, and spiritual healing work under my belt. And more to come. And when I look in my eyes, I see the teachers of my teachers, stretching back through time. The wounded healer knows how to heal because they've done the work themselves, and they share healing from a deep place. I'm grateful to be a wounded healer from this lineage. I'm grateful for what it took to get here. I wouldn't change a fucking thing.

Every soul needs to shine with authenticity. Everyone needs to heal from something. And there are many benefits from the darkest of times.

❦ What's possible for you, now that you've been through difficult times?

_____

_____

_____

_____

_____

_____

_____

_____

_____

_____

_____

_____

❦ Would you trade it for a smooth path, or did the struggle make you who you are today? If that struggle has turned into bitterness, resentment and/or anger, you need to dig deeper into that. My contact information is on indiazoe. com/contact ☺

_____

_____

_____

_____

_____

_____

_____

_____

_____

❦ Kids say and do the darndest things. Eli never hesitated to offer me money to continue in the game of monopoly. Where in your life do you have kindness for others without expectation?

_____

_____

_____

_____

_____

_____

_____

❦ How have you, or are you, healing your pain—physical, emotional, spiritual, and mental? How about we jot it all down here and release what your body is holding onto.

_____

_____

_____

_____

_____

_____

_____

_____

_____

_____

_____

_____

BURNING RITUAL
There is a beautiful burning ritual
for you at the end of this book.
Feel free to go there now,
or when it feels right
for you.
Burn, baby, burn—it!

15

THINGS LIKE THIS DON'T HAPPEN TO US

The news leads with stories of violence, destruction, and tragedy to prey on primal fears, and people watch through the lens of being sure things like *that* won't happen to *them*, until one day when it does. When violence touched my family and me, I learned that the root of suffering is unhealed trauma. Trauma leads to terrible things happening and increased suffering. It's what we bury and suppress that shows up in self-harm and harm to others, but I hadn't learned this yet because *things like that didn't happen to us.*

Every year in the United States, there are murders, stabbings, and rapes, but what is rarely discussed is the violence towards men that is inflicted by women. One in three women and one in four men experience some form of physical violence by an intimate partner. Every year, over 750,000 men are victims of domestic abuse. Statistics also show that over 50 percent of men do not talk about the abuse.

Healing comes in layers and stages. It's a big job. Many people think, "This horrible thing can't happen in *my* relationship, family, school, neighborhood, and country." But it does. Healing at the level of the soul starts when we develop a sense of self-worth, then we give ourselves the gift of healing.

I would never have imagined my life would be touched by violence and its aftermath. Our family had some funky communication issues. We didn't know how to work things out—but violence? Not possible. It was unimaginable until we had to deal with it.

Like all families, mine operated from our deepest unhealed wounds, unconscious conditioning, limited beliefs, and habitual patterns. The shadow-self is multilayered.

I didn't have a clue about how to deal with my feelings and emotions. There was nothing to provide spiritual structure, no wise teachers around. There was no guidance or access to information other than mainstream news in the 60s and 70s. This was before Oprah spoke openly about complex subjects on air and normalized talking about difficult things. There was no personal growth section in a bookstore, or even a bookstore anywhere near me – a library perhaps – I was in a transformation desert.

What I'm about to share are the kinds of secrets people keep hidden because there's a great deal of embarrassment and shame around them. I could skip this chapter and save face for our family, but we are only as sick as our secrets, and I'm committed to wellbeing. So, here it goes. First, I'll give you some context about my family.

Growing up, my parents worked hard to put food on the table. They worked hard to move into a house they always dreamed of having – nothing nice or fancy - but a house, not a tiny 800 square foot apartment anymore. There was no one to watch me when I got home from school earlier than my brothers did. Eventually, I went from school to ballet and gymnastics. I didn't care for either activity, but I spent a few years doing them because my parents needed somewhere for me to be.

At home, I felt totally alone. My school wasn't a challenging academic environment; it was a high school where the administrators, teachers, and students skated by, and no one cared much about the future. Most kids in my class weren't going to college due to lack of funds, lack of inspiration, or were just happy with where they were. I felt I was headed pretty much nowhere. I couldn't figure out what I'd be good at in life because there weren't many options, especially for girls. I had little hope about my future and too much idle time on my hands. My drinking and drug use really took off.

By the age of seventeen, I moved out of my parents' home. I was earning my own money, had a great job, and could fully support myself. I knew for certain it was time to pack my suitcase when after a night of dropping acid, drinking, and rolling home sick and high, I realized it was best if my parents didn't see the mess I was becoming. Nobody else in my family was gay or alcoholic or on drugs, so off I went with my shameful secrets.

When I was younger, my brother Randy occasionally got stuck babysitting me, and he didn't like it. As a young man in his early twenties, he had little interest in his little sister, and there was a chasm between us. Randy reluctantly took me with him to shoot photographs or watch him paint or show me his martial arts moves.

When I was 10 years old, Randy headed to law school. When I was 11, he came home and announced that he had quit law school and joined the Church of Scientology. There was a sense of alarm that filled the house. I was immediately sent to my bedroom. I knew Catholics and Mormons, but a church of science didn't seem like a big deal, so why were my parents so deeply distressed? I was only 11 years old, and it went over my head.

Emotions were suppressed. And we never spoke about it—ever. I didn't see or hear from my brother Randy for decades at a time. The first time he disappeared from the family was between 1990 and 1998, then he disappeared again in 2002 for 18 years—radio silence. To this day, five decades later, I am still unclear if Randy ever joined, or remained in the Church of Scientology, it was never spoken about, and I had forgotten all about it.

My brother Barry was closer to me in age, but he also wanted nothing to do with me. He was going through puberty, and all he cared about was baseball and girls. He had to make my lunch every day, and he seemed put out that I liked mustard and hated mayonnaise, but I was at his mercy. The mayonnaise he smeared on my sandwiches was sickeningly warm by lunch time. I was so grossed out I couldn't eat my sandwich, so I often went hungry until dinner.

Barry received his general contractor license by the age of nineteen and left home.

I missed him, even though I didn't know him well. As Barry and I matured into adults, we became very close; I could see he had his shortcomings, like all of us, but he was a thoroughly good guy, a solid man. Anyone who takes care of his mother at the end of her life the way my brother did has a lot of good in him. He operated from chivalry, helping stranded motorists or reaching the high shelf in the grocery store for someone who couldn't reach, or paying the dinner tab. He was attuned to being thoughtful and acted with consistency; you could count on him to be kind.

Barry purchased two acres of property in January 2016 in a small Oregon town where he had now lived for over twenty-five years. He was rebuilding the foundation in a very nice old home. He had just completed construction of a horse-training arena as a gift for his new wife, Mallory. While he worked on the house, they lived in the RV he hauled to construction sites when he had a big project. During construction of the house, the RV was planted on his property with stabilizers and utilities. He rode off on his Harley every morning to work in Portland.

I visited Oregon once or twice a year to see him and to spend quality time with my dear Aunt Charlotte on her five acres of property. One warm Sunday afternoon, I had an opportunity to go horseback riding with Mallory; it was a chance to get to know her better. They got married a year after they'd met so I didn't know her well.

We headed out on the horses, taking our time, chatting, and having fun as we rode up into the hills of Grande Ronde. We started our return just before sunset. We were nearing the property when suddenly, up the hill, two dogs erupted in fierce barking. My horse was already in a trot when he spooked, and my right foot slipped out of the stirrup; the dogs barked louder, my horse took off at a full fucking gallop.

The inside of my left thigh was the only thing in the saddle; my entire body was hanging off the right side of the horse like a Comanche warrior. A short distance behind me, Mallory yelled, "Haaaang ooonn Cheeeerryyyllll, haaaaaang ooonnn!" I gripped the saddle horn, reins, and the horse's mane, thinking, *This is not going to end well!* I could see myself landing hard on the side of my body that was healing from multiple surgeries. I was sure that if I fell, I'd split open like a ripe watermelon, or snap my neck. A waste of a body after all the work I'd done to keep it in one piece.

I somehow hit the stride of the horse at the perfect moment, pulled myself upright with all my strength and rode like bloody hell. Barry came outside to see what all the commotion was about, just as my horse galloped up to the RV. I anticipated the hard stop and held on with every muscle and sinew, rearing my body backward like a cowboy at a rodeo, so I wouldn't be thrown over the front of the horse. Mallory's horse galloped up beside me, and we looked at each other in disbelief. *What the fuck just happened?* We laughed so hard we nearly peed our pants and swung off the saddles, grateful to feel the solid ground beneath our feet.

Less than a month later, I got a frantic call. Barry had been stabbed by Mallory, who had been on probation for a year at this time. She had been taking drug tests, which were forcing her into sobriety. Shortly after her probation lifted, she came home blackout drunk. It was very late when Barry heard her coming into the RV; he was in bed in his T-shirt and boxers. He got up and sat at the bottom of the bed, confused by how she was behaving. He heard her walking away from the bedroom back into the kitchen. He sat and waited for a minute in the dark. He saw her approaching and knew something was off. Then he noticed she was holding a long knife in her hand, trying to hide it behind her forearm. As soon as she lifted her arm, he saw the glint of the knife blade as she attacked in fury, slashing at his chest, wrist, and belly.

He did a backward somersault on the bed, pulled out his handgun from the nightstand, pointed it at her forehead, and pulled the trigger. The gun didn't go off. She ran.

Barry called the Sheriff's office and paramedics. When they arrived, they told Barry that if she'd stabbed him just an inch in either direction, she would have killed him instantly. When the local sheriff saw a photo of Mallory, they recognized her. She'd been arrested several times under different last names, for DUIs and for domestic abuse of other men. She was currently serving one-year probation for a DUI—her fourth. Barry didn't know any of this.

In the courtroom, Barry heard for the first time that his new bride, had been married more times than he knew about and was currently associated with a known felon who was connected to the Aryan Brotherhood. With this new information, my brother was even more concerned about his safety. He decided to reboot his life with a long stay in Mexico.

I tried to talk to Barry about what he'd experienced, but he was still in shock. Still, I was sure that over time, we would sort it out together. I would be there for him to help him process what had happened and heal from it. Together, we could work this out even though *these kinds of things don't happen to us.*

What was it was like for Barry to be stabbed by someone he loved, for him to discover the destructive rage of the woman he had married? The trauma and the fundamental loss of trust must have shaken him to the core. Had he missed warning signs about his new wife? Because he was avoiding facing reality? How could things have gone so far off the deep end?

I supported my brother the best I could. He was healing from multiple stab wounds and the loss of the dream he'd been building with her. I was healing my shitstorm of body, mind, and finances. Together, we were healing from the chaos Mallory, a violent alcoholic, had created for everyone in her orbit.

I had a lot of compassion for Barry and for what he was going through. And I also had compassion for Mallory; I really did. I have been a blackout drunk many times. I have made dangerous choices. I have lost control. If I'd kept moving down a dark path, I could have ended up like her.

She was sent to prison with a six-year sentence for assault with a deadly weapon—she served three. I wondered what it would take for her to find redemption and forgiveness for herself and find a life of sobriety.

*

I was grateful that Barry and I were very connected to each other. We were authentic and raw, we shared openly and honestly about everything. I had a friend and brother in Barry. And then the phone rang. I heard words I couldn't comprehend. Barry had died with no warning. It was of natural causes.

I still see his trusting face in others, and I'm sad our brother Randy wasn't a part of Barry's life at the end. To this day, I miss Randy being a part of my life, and it's odd to know he's out there in the world, but we're not connected in a meaningful way. From all these things, I learned there are many opportunities to heal and do better. From this, I learned *trauma happens to all of us,* and it's an opportunity to feel compassion and create connection.

We can't always choose what happens to us, but we can *always* choose how we react to it. We can always choose to burn and rise from the ashes. We can always choose to move toward healing. You can be sure that the seeds of your greatness were planted in the shit of your soil.

For a time after Barry died, I shared what happened to our family from a victim's position. I'd watch people feel the shock of it as I told them what had happened. For a time, telling the story in a particular way was something I needed to make his loss real. I had to talk about what Mallory had done and learn not to worry about how our family would be judged. I shared it the way I did to become accustomed to telling the truth without leaving out things that were shameful and embarrassing and so very sad. I practiced not being attached to what someone might think.

But then I noticed the way I told the story got stuck, and I needed to unstick it. There are often hidden payoffs for remaining in the cycle of dysfunction and constriction, so look for them. Does telling your tale repeatedly do anything for you? Do you find yourself looping in your story, making you unable to be who you'd like to become? These are some challenges we face when it comes to our shadow. We are directly creating chaos, drama, and toxicity because of our lack of awareness in our storytelling. When this continues, it becomes a pattern, then a way of life.

What could open up for you if you trust Spirit, even when "bad things" happen? The false idea that everyone is supposed to be perfect, nothing is supposed to go "wrong," and nobody should have bad things happen to them will set you up for a life of complaining and a lack of creative problem solving. If you can be OK with anything that happens, you've got real power.

Once you face reality and understand you are empowered to heal, release, and rise, you can tell the complete truth in a way that transforms your life and models that for others. We all share the dark struggles, so we might as well share the breakthroughs too.

We all have circumstances in our family that we're not proud of, let alone want to share them with others. But if we get honest with ourselves and others, this can be the beginning of setting ourselves free.

❧ Do you take any pleasure in seeing someone else's life as a trainwreck to make yourself feel better about your life?

_____

_____

_____

_____

_____

_____

_____

_____

❧ Make a list of what has happened to you that you think *shouldn't have* happened to you.

❧ Look at the list of difficult times, the breakdowns, misfortunes, and catastrophes, and be with them. Give yourself time to process each one to see what's there. Growth can get stuck when the default belief is that it shouldn't have happened. Imagine that these life situations hadn't occurred, and that life had gone smoothly. What do you notice? What would you have missed out on learning if you didn't experience these big challenges?

_____

_____

_____

_____

_____

_____

_____

BURNING RITUAL
There is a beautiful burning ritual
for you at the end of this book.
Feel free to go there now,
or when it feels right
for you.
Burn, baby, burn—it!

16

RESPONSIBILITY DOESN'T SUCK

We tend to hang on to what we know because it's familiar, and it feels comfortable. The insanity of this is that even when our beliefs and behaviors are not serving us, we continue to cause ourselves emotional, mental, and physical harm. We imagine ways to postpone healing or turn a blind eye to the need to change because we are afraid of what it is we do not know. It's too easy to blame others and our circumstances. It's too easy to ignore what we alone are responsible for transforming.

When someone asks me, "What's the first step to moving forward?" I invite them to see going *back* is easy; it's the unknown of the future that can appear difficult. Living in the past is tempting and easier, so it's comfortable to roll around in the muck of it, but it's also easy to get stuck in the drama of it, and that drama holds an energy that will spiral downward and suck the life right out of your existence. Believe it or not, we have options. We have the opportunity to course correct and control our futures—ones that are created from imagination, curiosity, openness, purpose, and endless possibilities. Ask me how I know this!

There is no need to continue reengaging with the harmful past, like a dog returning to eat its vomit. We can be self-responsible, and I mean 100 percent responsible, to acknowledge with grace what life throws at us, and that means leaning into a new future—a future we have a say in creating.

Until we have experienced hardship, it's hard to comprehend how things can spiral so far down for someone else. It's human nature to believe in the myth of control. I've heard people describe control as the ultimate addiction. It's common in the world of light workers. *If I eat the right things, think the right thoughts, pray, and meditate the right way, nothing bad can ever happen to me or those I love, and my life will be nothing but unicorns shitting rainbows.* I'm exaggerating, but only a little.

The idea that we can use magical thinking and endless positive responses to everything to make it all go our way is enticing, even intoxicating, until the house burns down around us. Then we either hurt ourselves, self-destruct, flip from victim to perpetrator or perpetrator to victim, eat or drink excessively, cause emotional harm to our family or co-workers, do harmful drugs, spend money unwisely, get lost in the rabbit hole of social media, drift away in the world of THC gummies, or watch mind-numbing amounts of TV, anything to distract ourselves and disassociate from the reality of our painful existence. Let's not forget the parent who runs one to two kids to twelve different after school activities a week – that's a big distraction.

All these choices, and all of this grasping for a false sense of control, come from our unhealed self, the wounds that have bound you where you are. We continue into adulthood, bringing these unhealed parts of ourselves with us. These aspects of us are often the only place we operate and respond from, especially when triggered. Where do we begin? With responsibility. And responsibility doesn't suck.

*

Our culture encourages people to try to get out of taking responsibility for their actions. The default is to plead *not guilty* instead of accepting the consequences and impact of our actions with integrity. I love this one: how many illegal driving moves have you made? Then you find yourself in that moment of getting pulled over, and what happens? You're angry, justifying, complaining, and trying to get out of the ticket (that you caused) instead of owning the responsibility and moving the fuck on. Instead, you tell twelve of your closest friends what an asshole the cop was, and away we go.

I notice that even the insurance card tucked in the glove compartment of my car provides this unfortunate guidance, "When in an accident, do not admit fault." If I'm driving too fast in unsafe conditions and slide into another driver, I had better admit fault—on the spot—because it *was* my fault. To live with integrity differs from living with the mentality of, *What can I get away with?* You need to be asking yourself questions of integrity from within.

What is it like for perpetrators who know they are *guilty* to plead *not guilty* and fight to avoid accountability? This lack of grit keeps them from experiencing the remorse that could set their soul free and offer the possibility of real healing for their victim, themselves, and all concerned.

What is it like for victims who let what happened to them define who they are for the rest of their days? Persisting and thriving moves them into a powerful way of BEing, even after something dreadful has happened.

If we're causing harm, being critical, blaming others, and full of rage and anger, we can't become expressive, curious, and collaborative. If we're overly responsible and sacrificing, we're blocked from becoming a compassionate, encouraging individual who has iron-clad boundaries. If we get stuck in a victim consciousness of helplessness, dependence, and irresponsibility, we can't become someone who is grateful, vulnerable, and accountable.

Making those moves is our challenge, and no one can do it for us. What if we became personally and radically accountable, responsible for our emotional reactivity, our thoughts, our beliefs, our actions, and the way we impact others?

I know of a life coach who had a client who was clever and entitled. After the client could not follow through on commitments and repeatedly sabotaged his life, the coach probed into the underlying cause of these behaviors. The client finally confessed that he had killed his first wife many years ago and had gotten away with it. Completely. There was no chance he'd ever be caught for her murder. At the level of his soul, he knew this wasn't right. The rest of his life would have been lived in the shadow of his guilt, shame, and remorse. So, the coach did a phenomenal thing and worked with the client to prepare him to take responsibility for his actions.

The client walked into a police station to turn himself in. He plead guilty and served his time. He made the restitution he could. He dedicated the rest of his life to something better, and he emerged from prison a different man. He was no longer a man who had hidden and lied and succeeded at getting away with murder, but one who had the courage to face the consequences and impact of his actions. It blows my mind that this level of commitment to accountability is possible.

Becoming radically responsible is the direction our culture needs to take, and I'm grateful to be on the front lines. I love being a part of that change. And to help support it, I must be vigilant myself, or the tricks of the ego can spin me out. Imagine what it would be like if we grew the fuck up and freed ourselves! Being free from the anguish of the past is real freedom. I'm passionate about causing this level of transformation and helping people face themselves and rise from the ashes. Some of us are burned in the fire, while others remake ourselves in it.

What are the choices that have gotten you right here, right now? There's no spiritual bypass for this work—no shortcuts. Take some time to write your answers to these questions. Releasing the burdens that keep you in the realm of your shadow is deep work. So let's get in there and excavate, discovering these hidden treasures within you.

❦ Let's look at your choices. Do you burn down your house to transform yourself? Or do you succumb to your past behaviors and end up burnt to a crisp?

_____

_____

_____

_____

❦ What are the secrets that hold you hostage?

_____

_____

_____

❦ Where do you lie to cover things up? Where do you leave out the truth to mislead people?

_____

_____

_____

_____

❧ What do you think you gain when you dodge responsibility?

❧ If you're not ready, what are you waiting for? What do you gain by staying stuck – how's that working out for you?

_____

_____

_____

_____

_____

_____

_____

_____

BURNING RITUAL
There is a beautiful burning ritual
for you at the end of this book.
Feel free to go there now,
or when it feels right
for you.
Burn, baby, burn—it!

17

AROUND THE BONFIRE

My brother Barry didn't wake up on September 1st, 2016, thinking it was the last time he'd see the sunrise or the sunset; he was 59 years young. His affairs were in order. With his impending divorce finalized, so we thought, and with Mallory in prison for assault, my family pulled together to handle what was needed, getting his belongings back to the lien holders: his RV, a Harley, and his dually pickup, the remnants we all leave behind when we go home.

A small group of family and friends gathered on a beach on the Oregon coast for a ceremony to say goodbye. I pushed my feet deep into the sand, so I'd feel grounded. I was sad and felt completely alone amongst family. Barry hadn't died at the hands of Mallory and her knife, but from natural causes. It was hard for me to accept he was gone. Losing my brother was a jolt that caused my world to shift from healing my body to the healing of my spirit.

Hearing the water lapping on the shoreline with the wind blowing off the water, we said goodbye to Barry. I was reminded that my life was not an endless resource. We all know this intellectually, but we don't *really* get it until something big happens. Then the reality of life and death sets in. The time is now. Listen to the fire in your belly. Make it count.

I almost met with death in 2012 from cancer. I lost Barry just when I was rediscovering and reinventing myself. I had been stripped so much of my personality, the ego, that I was raw and numb, and I knew it would take a special coach to help me with where I was in my life at that point in time.

On the rugged, uphill path of life, there are bonfires to warm us along the way, people to put an arm around us and care for us—family, friends, lovers, partners, colleagues, community to teach us about communication, forgiveness, and love. We fall short; we course correct and continue on. We shift. We pivot. We reset. We cultivate. We surrender. We offer support to fellow travelers. What do we get out of doing all this work? Really? What do we *really* get out of all this? Continue reading to find out! It's magical, mystical, and so much fun!

*

I had come across potential coaches throughout the previous year, but nobody felt right until the day I was in a workshop at The Soul of Yoga, in Encinitas, California on a sunny Sunday afternoon. The woman leading us sang sacred kirtan music and played the harmonium, and we joined her in movement and song, it was rock and roll mixed with Devine devotion like nothing I'd ever experienced! The mood was playful, fun, and full of life force! She exuberated this essence about her that I couldn't wrap my head around, but I could feel it - it was pure joy.

We moved through our workshop, transported by the feeling of aliveness. *Shakti,* the divine power to create, destroy, and create again. Shakti, the fierce feminine warrior of love and light. The authenticity, wildness, vulnerability, and depth I was looking for filled the room, and I smiled as my surgery-scarred body moved freely. The music moved me.

After the workshop concluded, a small group of us formed a healing circle, and a woman asked for support for healing from breast cancer. I swung my head around, "Oh my God, me, too. I'm still healing from the aftermath of treatment." A kind man spoke up, "I am an oncology researcher. Let me share what I know that could be helpful." From there, we dove into a deep conversation about healing from both the medical and mystical perspective. I settled in and relaxed, knowing I was in the right place, at the right time, with the right people.

The woman who had sung so beautifully that day is a transformational coach, teacher, and recording artist who performs original sacred music and is known for getting thousands of people on their feet and in their hearts to raise their spiritual vibration. Her name is Larisa.

When the healing circle closed and we were all going our separate ways, I got into a conversation with her about transformation. She gave me her contact information, and I scheduled my first session with her two weeks later. It was imperative for my healing process to include taking stock of my thinking, believing, feeling, and operating, and I became determined to create a different way of living away from the anger that engulfed me.

*

With all the yoga classes, workshops, and retreats that I had been attending, I'd been learning along the way about being *in the heart*. I heard this phrase a lot but couldn't figure out how to get there. See the problem already? It's not a *thinking* thing, it's a *feeling* thing. How could I be in my heart when I'd been an emotionally shut down jackass who could only operate from ego and anger?

I've done my apprenticeship in areas that are on the cutting edge of science and spirituality. I have a daily plan for how I continue to learn and evolve. There are so many ways I get support. Are you open to receiving support from even higher realms? It's all there, ready for you to tap into a new way of living created for spiritual evolution and personal growth.

As I became (and still work to become) a spiritual adult listening to inner wisdom, the greater wisdom that comes from spirit becomes a priority. I met my first Shaman, Chiara, also at The Soul of Yoga, who guided me towards plant medicine. I started working regularly with her and plant medicine and with Larisa on the cognitive and behavioral part of my work. I sat regularly with my shaman in a sacred, intentional setting, using plant medicine.

Various medicinal plants are available, and psylocibin is the medicine I connect with the most. When dosed at my ceremonial level, plants offer me what I refer to as my truth serum; they reveal the parts of myself that need to be seen, healed, and integrated. It's deep work and also very beautiful.

From my point of view, the person who can explain it best is Michael Pollan in his books *How To Change Your Mind* and *This is Your Mind On Plants* and the television series *How To Change Your Mind,* which you'll find on a well-known streaming platform. If the world of plant medicine is new to you, wait until you feel the intuitive wisdom about where, when, and with whom to sit in sacred ceremony. You may never feel the pull toward that experience; it's not necessary for your growth but it will accelerate the process.

In the 21st Century, we are rediscovering wisdom that has always been with us on the planet. Many cultures have honored the tradition, while others overlooked it. Plant medicine is a fertile place to go for growth and evolution. This is the complete opposite of partying; it's a high level of spiritual practice when approached in ceremony. It's an entry point to amazing breakthroughs, and CEOs of successful companies, activists, scientists, artists, entrepreneurs, teachers, and healers are bringing it into mainstream culture.

*

I had been working with plant medicine for a year at that point, and there is a process of integration; it can show up on the day of the ceremony or years later. And it shows up in a variety of ways.

In the fall of 2017, I headed to Nashville for some glamping. One morning, in the tent with the flaps open on both sides, I could see and take in the fall colors and the crispness of the air, and I found myself on my knees and became aware that my body had its wisdom about how to move. When my mind was quiet, my body naturally bowed to the Divine in devotion. I sobbed with relief and gratitude. My body intuitively rocked forward touching my forehead to the ground, then my body rocked back to sit straight, then rocked forward, with my forehead touching the ground again. This automatic movement went on for what seemed like a long time; something was shifting, and I could feel it in every cell of my body. I had surrendered to what was at the time.

The Mantra I was singing along with was about compassion, grace, and spreading light and love. It became my prayer, my self-expression. I was in Divine presence, and I felt it profoundly. My entire BEing had been taken over by the wisdom of my body. I felt full of grace, and suddenly, I felt pulled to hop on a plane to visit my Aunt Charlotte.

I love spending time with my Aunt Charlotte. She lives alone and manages a house and five acres of pasture, berry patch, and garden by herself and has since my uncle died 24 years ago. She's 91 years young and so physically strong it's shocking. I've watched her climb into the bucket of her John Deere tractor and raise herself up to clean the gutters of the house.

I want to be like my Aunt Charlotte when I grow up, to love life like she does, to stay creative and productive until the end. She is a master gardener, who lives mostly off the land, eating what she grows. When I'm on the property, I enjoy doing things for and with her. On my last trip, I cleaned, sanded, and painted a 200-foot fence. Together, we pull weeds, trim vines, and gather many pounds of fresh berries—marionberries, tayberries, raspberries, blueberries, and blackberries. Do you know the satisfaction that comes from accomplishing something that can be easily measured—like berry picking?

My version of driving a tractor and picking berries is transforming families and individuals in the darkest nights, working with executives in evolving their companies, conducting workshops, ceremonies, retreats, and making sacred objects to remind people of their transformational deaths and rebirths. Nothing is more joyful and meaningful to me than being invited to help turn around a life, a family, a company, or a team, and seeing the result of change—collaboration, connection, cohesiveness, compassion, support, and purpose.

If I live into my 90s, that's where you'll find me, with my sleeves rolled up wearing a hat, getting shit done, and ready for the next exciting thing.

*

So many people are full of complaints, opinions, and excuses and use those distractions to not get anything done. I confess it bores the ever-living shit out of me when I occasionally slip into a pattern of excuses or overwhelm, or when I'm around those who live in that limited world. Just the thought of a mediocre life makes my skin crawl.

This irritability with constraint is a good thing. It's productive to be agitated by Divine discontent, which differs greatly from making excuses, whining, and complaining. Snakes get cranky before they shed the skin they've outgrown. Their eyes cover with a milky film, and they become lethargic.

Just underneath this death of the old is a sleek and shiny new skin that fits the new life of the snake. To enjoy that rebirth, they must first struggle to shed the old. It's not pleasant. They get pissed off. They scrape their bodies against rocks and branches to pull off the old skin. They writhe and slide. And the irritation leads to a big breakthrough.

For me, wriggling out of the skin is a soulful preference. It's how I'm put together. And my hunger for transformation extends to supporting my clients in wriggling out of theirs.

In this dance with Spirit, in this wriggling out of the old skin, nothing of life is wasted. Everything we've learned so far goes to fuel the fire of our transformation and create our rebirth into a powerful new life. I'm able to be there for people during their toughest times because I have experienced and integrated transformational methodologies at a very deep level and will continue to until the end. And I go through this cycle continually. I teach it, and then—*wham!* —I'm back in a process myself. There is no coming into our true purpose and potential without facing ourselves, and it's hard because every step-up means burning away the old version of ourselves.

I don't observe situations, people, or places from right-wrong, good-bad, black-white, this or that; I let them flow in nonattachment. This is something I have practiced since 2009 and only adds to gaining the momentum in sovereignty. To make out a behavior, a person, or a situation as "bad," is insinuating it's wrong—no. It presented itself. It's there, it happened, you chose it, or whatever the case may be because it's part of the medicine, the teaching. It's when we label it that causes the conflict. All situations and all things at all times are exactly as they should be otherwise, they'd be different.

It is within your reach to be in the place where you transcend the ordinary world and come fully to life on this extraordinary planet. It's something we all have as our birthright—to belong here and to be of service to what breaks our hearts and provides our bliss. That's the sweet spot. Seeing what needs to be transformed and feeling your part in what there is to do about it. The good hard work of transformation. The best work there is!

In this chapter, I shared about attachment to good-bad, right-wrong, etc. plant medicine, mediocracy, and shedding of old skin. In my humble opinion, non-attachment is one of the most important topics in this chapter because it's a limiting way to live. When we constrict ourselves to labels, we then ultimately must unpack those labels in order to expand our mind, the energy and how we perceive things (to name a few).

❧ Can you identify in your life where you attach labels to situations? Example: if you're an addict (in recovery or active) you see everything you're doing as, "fucked up," "wrong," and "bad." Subsequently, you're feeding - energetically, mentally, and emotionally – how bad you *already* feel about yourself! However, everything that you're experiencing brings *value* to who you are becoming. It's the teachings that are necessary for growth and transformation.

_____

_____

_____

_____

_____

_____

❧ Can you be open to being open to non-attachment? Maybe try it for 15, 30 or 45 days and see how it feels, how it flows with you.

❧ Who is your coach for this part of the journey?

_____

_____

_____

_____

_____

❧ Where are your moments of simple joy in good work found?

❧ When do you feel most aligned with what you are doing?

_____

_____

_____

_____

_____

❧ List anything you can tell is currently in your way and give it to the flames!

_____

_____

_____

_____

_____

You have been shedding *your skin* through the processes in this book. You're well on your way!

BURNING RITUAL
There is a beautiful burning ritual
for you at the end of this book.
Feel free to go there now,
or when it feels right
for you.
Burn, baby, burn—it!

18

THE BOOBY TRAP

After an entire year of treatments—six treatments of chemo, a mastectomy, and 32 treatments of radiation in 2012—I was tired. Just tired. I was still working with my client in Arkansas and was bouncing between Tennessee, California and Arkansas for almost a year. In September 2013, I was worn to a nub physically and emotionally and not firing on all cylinders. I had that doomsday feeling again, the same darkness I had experienced when it all crashed down upon me in 2008 and 2009. I was fucking miserable and working for a boss who I felt was throwing me under the bus at every stop along the route. It was emotionally painful, and I did not handle it well at all.

Over the next year, I would put on a whopping 60 pounds, and all I could do was be a *victim*, rationalizing or justifying situations seemingly happening to me, not for me. My boss's behavior and treatment toward me should have been my opportunity to move on, but I didn't have the capacity, mindset, understanding, or knowledge to know at the time I was in victim-consciousness or victimhood. And I allowed the fear of finances to make my decisions for me.

It would take several more years before I completely understood how conditioned I had become through my upbringing, AA, past relationships, society, or culture. All I thought was, *You did this or that to me, and now I am the victim of your misguided behavior and personal issues.* It was painful, so painful. I carried that story and angst about my boss for several years, and boy howdy was I up in her grill. I had never blown up in size like that before, and all I did was blame my insanity on my external environment.

In January 2015, I took three months off work to head to San Diego to have my breast reconstructive surgery. I was not a candidate for implants because of the third-degree radiation burns on my right chest wall, and I settled for my only option—DIEP flap process. They used my belly fat and belly skin to make a breast. I was scheduled for seven surgeries total and ended up with ten because of severe complications that would throw a wrench into my life once again.

The complications from the DIEP flap were intense and forced me into a situation in which I would have to abruptly quit my job in Arkansas and stay in California. In the middle of this, my wallet was stolen, and my dog, Bodhi, was killed by a car while under the care of a friend back in Arkansas. I was fucking distraught. He was the love of my life and I would lose my medical insurance due to an error on my part while in the middle of surgeries! It was a cluster fuck and a shit show, and I was falling deeper and deeper into that same darkness that seemed all too familiar.

*

Wow, gifts are showing up! These are different gifts from those we bring into this lifetime. The gifts I am speaking of here are the presents that show up in all my affairs, even when ungraceful and roaming aimlessly. I had a huge connection of dots regarding contracts and agreements one night as I was lying in bed about to fall asleep. I have no recollection of what prompted the insight, when suddenly, I sat straight up and took in a gasp of air. *Oh my God, she's (my old boss) done her part. If she wasn't so mean to me, I would not have eaten my emotions and gained 60 pounds. I needed those 60 pounds of flesh and fat to have a breast.*

I sat there, stunned and elated. Yes, yes, yes! I got it. There was no other way I would have medically been able to have reconstructive surgery unless it was the DIEP Flap. We needed the fat and the belly skin to make the breast. I could forgive her and set her free as well as myself at that moment. I have nothing but grace and complete gratitude now for the journey to awareness of understanding contracts and agreements at the soul level. We make these agreements long before we incarnate. We don't remember them, just like we don't remember anything else, like the fact that we chose this life, at this time, with these teachings and lessons. I discovered what was Truth for me; this is the path I have been on ever since—the path of my Soul's evolution.

In my process, I held that angst, energy, anger, and resentment towards my boss for *several* years. Where in your life are you holding on to anger, resentment, justification and obsessing over the story, confirming, and validating your shortcomings?

✎ Reflect on your life, on the negative emotions you hold towards others. I invite you to look at the situation from a higher perspective/observer role. Are you able to see how that person/situation was there *for* you? If not… indiazoe.com/contact ☺

BURNING DOWN THE HOUSE

19

TO BENEFIT OTHERS

I needed a trip, a vacation, to go somewhere, anywhere—anywhere being India, Bali, Thailand, or any other country far, far away that offered yoga. I hadn't had a vacation since 2011, and it was March 2016; I was eager and needed to go. But I rationalized I couldn't since I wasn't working.

Like many of us, I could only see value in money, not value in my emotional needs. We often lack self-care because we're so busy paying bills and surviving over all other needs, when taking care of ourselves is just as important—if not more. I spent months going back and forth with myself, trying to rationalize taking time away. I was burned the fuck out. I believed that because I wasn't working, I shouldn't take time to separate myself from it all and find space to relax and convalesce.

At the last minute, I remembered I had a lot of frequent flyer miles and ended up heading to Goa, India 12 days later—first class. I got my shit together, and away I went.

My room was simple, beautiful, and affordable. The walls were ocean blue and blood orange. I focused on spiritual practice, connection to nature, healthy food, restorative sleep, and deep transformation and healing.

When I went to a temple to pray, my body and face showed the ravages of cancer treatments and surgeries. My fuzzy duck hair was still growing back, and I had limited eyebrows, dark circles under my eyes, and no eyelashes. I walked slowly and cautiously. Some little girls, around the age of six to ten, were drawn to me and were curious about my appearance. I explained I had been very sick. Their instant compassion was a balm to my soul. They climbed onto my lap and draped their arms around my shoulders. We whispered and laughed in the quiet of the temple, and I smiled at all of them and saw that *love* was everywhere. I sat and enjoyed the little ones giggling around me, the flowers on the altar, and the cracked soles of my bare feet. And I loved myself as I was.

The retreat location was a short distance from a bridge spanning the Mandrem River. I walked through the sand, beyond the huts, and there was the Arabian Sea. With my feet sinking into the warm sand at the shoreline, I filled my lungs with my first deep breath in a very long time.

I got down to basics—four hours of yoga a day and meals cooked in the outdoor kitchen. I ate as if for the first time, appreciating every bite that fueled my body. I walked around connecting with strangers and learned I could be anywhere in the world and find a spot of grace with others and all alone. I let myself fall in love with the soul of everyone I saw. I surrendered. I loved my body. I embraced my essence.

But I was still floating in life, not drowning, not swimming, but floating, just enough to keep my head above water and not completely drown emotionally. I was incredibly lonely, just being with myself completely. It was a place where one does not even recognize themselves. I started going to weekly sessions with my coach, Larisa, when I got back; I was still stuck in being a victim to circumstances that were haunting me from breast cancer - losing my medical insurance, failing to file my taxes on time, my credit went to shit, and still had the expenses I had before having to quit my job, still trying to overcome the real estate crash. It was so emotionally painful. I had no words to express the state I was in.

*

In 2017, I came to a whole body, mind, spirit, and energy awareness—finally! Over the years, I had heard the words, "Don't be a victim," but I didn't really understand what that meant. I eventually came to understand that I am an Energy Being, experiencing myself in physical form, but before that, I had caused all my pain and deep suffering.

All I did in the past was follow what was dictated to me by others until I found myself years later in turmoil and crises. This was ultimately when I became aware of just how much conditioning and programming, I had received outside of my family structure and those around me who were in the same state of awareness (or lack of it). I just kept doing what we are all trained to do—grow up, go to college, find a mate, have kids, and go into debt.

A major turning point for me came one day in Spring 2017 when I had a session with my coach. She went through her opening ritual and prayers, allowing for Spirit to guide her in her session work. We were sitting knee to knee, and she looked at me, tilted her head, was quiet for a moment, and said, "Hmm, they're telling me you have done your work here and that you don't need to be here any longer if you don't want to be!"

I was taken aback! I leaned in and said, "What did you just say?"

"They're telling me you have done your work here at this level and that you don't need to be here any longer if you don't want to be! Does this make sense to you?" She said with her head tilted, confused, and bewildered.

I started bawling. "I am done! I am fucking tired! I am fucking exhausted! I just can't keep going on like this. I don't

140

want to go on living anymore!" The cat was out of the bag, and there was no going back now.

None of my new friends, my new connections, had known anything about my life as it once had been—who I was, what I achieved, my career, my accomplishments, or how I got there. They all met me during the darkest, graceless, fucking messy, and unforgiving time of my life, and all that happened was that I was so welcomed, loved, cared for, and supported in every way possible by those who chose to want to connect with me. I knew I had now found my tribe, even though I was a disaster on so many levels.

There was such a vast difference in acceptance, or the lack of it, from my prior life. And this included my own lack of acceptance. In the past, I thought and believed that I knew your path better than you did and, therefore, judged with contempt from my viewpoint, and what a limited view point it was!

At the end of my three-hour session, I was instructed to go home and feel into what I wanted to do. If my choice was to stay on the planet, I would have to get into much deeper work to understand the disdain I held towards institutions.

I had no fight left in me. I really wanted to go, to depart the planet. I had nothing left in me—nothing! It had gotten so bad that I was sleeping upwards of 10 to 14 hours a day and would often not even brush my teeth for days on end. I didn't even care if they all fell out. For those last few years, I had lost all *hope* and didn't have any idea how I would ever find any again. That was my truth—my painful truth.

For the next few days following my session, I would stare at myself in the mirror and ponder my way out, asking myself if I had the guts to just let go and depart. I was in a desperate place.

Almost a week had gone by since my session. I was standing in the shower and just started bawling. I asked myself,

Should I stay or go? This is my out *right now. Do I have the guts to leave?* I had no family, a few friends, no fun, no adventure, minimal love of self, and a lot of sadness. So yes, I wanted to depart my physical body. While the hot water was gently coming down the top of my head and thinning itself on my face and neck, I was crying, wondering what the hell I needed to do to change, let go, shift, anything!

Before I knew it, I was lying in the tub with the water still running on my body. I must have been there for 45 minutes, just crying and crying; it was cathartic yet again. The next afternoon, I stood in my small bathroom, looking in the mirror, which is difficult to do when you lack self-love, but I asked myself, *What message are you sending to the Universe if you were to leave? Would it mean your experiences are all for nothing—for you and others? Can anyone benefit from your journey? And what about the gifts that were promised?*

I wasn't expecting a new car; that's for sure, but I was curious to know what would be *equal to or greater than the pain I was in.* I'd experienced yet another deep surrender—the need to control. I had done a tremendous amount of self-work. It had been messy, ungraceful, and full of anger, but I kept trudging.

I didn't set out on some spiritual path toward enlightenment, awareness, or consciousness; rather, I was kicked all the way down the path due to my choices, beliefs, conditioning, and living outside myself. Finally, humility rang my doorbell. I knew I was not more powerful than the Universe, and if I didn't live my life differently, I was going to suffer even more. And there wasn't much room left—if any.

What I had been learning was about being in the heart. This I could understand. Dropping from my head to my heart had been something I had been working on but traveling that short distance between the two took a rather long time for me—five years, to be exact.

I went back to my coach for a session two weeks later. "What decision have you made?" she asked.

"I feel and believe that my experiences could benefit others, maybe keep them from harming themselves or another. Or perhaps, they too have lost all hope, and I can help show them there is, in fact, another way or other ways to work through all the pain through my journey to hell and back!"

The cat was fully out of the bag, and the burden of it released. Where in your life can you let the cat out of the fucking bag? This is one of the shortest chapters in the book and probably the most important!

_____

_____

_____

_____

ò   Who is in your current tribe?
If you don't have a tribe yet, let your growth show you the way.

ò   Are you willing to give up "waiting for" and *BE* who you truly are, doing what you love to do? Is your life full of play and purpose? If not, how can you make it so?

_____

_____

_____

_____

20

EXPERIENCES LIKE NO OTHER

I n the fall of 2017, I started helping as Larisa's assistant in exchange for a ticket for the five-day event at Bhakti Fest. I wanted and needed to be of service, here, there, and everywhere. Working in conjunction with plant medicine, a coach, and my self-work all helped to manage my emotions, as well as the darkness and loss of hope I had been experiencing for several years.

My shaman, Chiara, and I set out for five days to Joshua Tree, California, headed to Bhakti Fest. We set up our cabin to prepare for our plant medicine ceremony and for receiving a few other friends of ours - Joday, Billy, Leela, Jason and others. We always arrive a day early, before a festival starts to partake in ceremony prior to the festival beginning. We set our intention, clarity, openness, and responsibility and into ceremony we went.

It was just the previous month, that I had participated in sacred medicine in sacred space for the first time. My personal medicine journeys were always facilitated by my shaman.

Until that time, I didn't really know much about medicines of the earth except Ayahuasca, and I didn't try any until almost ten years after I left AA. I wasn't seeking a drug fix, rather how to deepen myself even further. If I was seeking a fix of the drug variety, I assure you, it would have come a long, long, long time earlier.

It's the same with cannabis; for me, personally, it is not about escaping my reality. The benefit for me is that it takes me deep into my subconscious, where I can access my higher-self and receive downloads that are not yet available in my conscious mind. It also helps me stay off pharmaceuticals that have horrible side effects.

I met Joday on my first Bali trip in 2016, she became a dear friend of mine, and still is. On this night at Bhakti Fest, we were all coming out of our medicine and Joday, in all her medicine-woman wisdom, put her hand on my back, and I just went into a deep backbend. All this white light was pouring into my heart, pouring in, pouring in, pouring in, and when it stopped, I dropped to my knees and started laughing. "What the fuck just happened?!" I asked, laughing and stunned at the same time. I had been doing all this work to *live in my heart,* but I was still coming from my mind, in this moment, I knew I was making the descension from mind to heart, while *ascending* my consciousness. I knew Joday and Chiara were trying to open me up! They did. And I was ready.

This opening was the beginning of the immense healing I was about to embark on so many levels: the physical, emotional, spiritual, and the ethereal bodies.

Shortly after returning home from Joshua Tree, I attended a free breathwork workshop at the Soul of Yoga. I discovered through this amazing breath-work class that I can astral travel by leaving my body and floating out into the galaxy. Yeah, I wouldn't have believed it either until I experienced it!

I was flying high on life; I couldn't even believe the complete 180-degree turn my life had taken. Three days after the workshop, I headed back to Bali, Indonesia, for a fifteen-day yoga retreat with Larisa and 20 others—my second time.

There were a handful of others who also returned from the 2016 group.

I could not have anticipated, dreamed up, or created the experiences that were about to unfold in the next 48 hours. The retreat itself was amazing, the connections I still have are priceless, and I felt the endless beauty of Bali: all the Temples we visited, the orphanage we spent a day at connecting beautifully with the children, the Monkey Dance, the Waterfalls, and the endless side adventures. An awesome side adventure took place one evening when we were out in the beauty of darkness in the Indian Ocean. The moon was shimmering off the water; the air was clear, and it was quiet except for the three of us playing. We were in the water for about 20 minutes when I put my foot down on what felt like a porcupine. It was painful!

I stepped on a sea urchin—ouch! I wouldn't put my feet down for the next 30 minutes we were in the water. I just kept saying, "Fuck, this hurts!" My two friends were asking if I wanted to get out of the water. "No! But it fucking hurts! It feels like I stepped on a porcupine!"

I had one of my friends carry me out of the water on her back, she's six inches shorter than me, and we were naked and laughing our assess off. I refused to put my feet down. We got help from the retreat center and woke up a nurse who had been on our retreat. My two friends hung out with me for hours while each of the little splinters from the urchin was tweezed. What an adventure! We even posted about it on social media.

The next morning, several other friends had posted inquires to me, "I wonder what sea urchin medicine is in India?" For the first time, I noticed the harmony of Mother Nature, not the incident of, "Look what happened *to* me! I stepped on a sea urchin." Instead, I opened my mind and heart and inquired about the sea urchin (spirit) medicine:

Teaches discernment and the art of underlying circumstances. Slow and methodical, she shows how to maneuver with tenacity and patience. Nothing is impossible when Urchin is guiding you. Do you have a tough exterior and a soft inside? Urchin will teach this balance of rough and tender. She teaches ways of extracting information out of the rubble of the mind and of the day-to-day activities.

This was when I made the connection of how disconnected I was to Mother Earth. It was eye opening.

When the retreat concluded, five of us went to another part of Bali for an extra four days to decompress and have some fun. Not all of us had a reservation, but we made it work—girls in one lodge and the boys in another.

After we all settled in, we gathered in the private courtyard when I realized Larisa was moving into Kundalini, which is a life-force (or liberation of energy), meaning it's a major source of internal power. It's within all of us, but not all of us have experienced it as an *awakening*. It's thought in the traditional teaching to be feminine (known as Kundalini Shakti) and can only flow freely when one's chakras are open and clear.

Before I knew it, we were all in an energy dance—pure energy—sitting anywhere from five to ten feet from each other on the ground, spread about in the courtyard. At that point in time, I just kept staying with the energy and trying not to go into my head, trying to figure it out! It was a beautiful, mind-blowing experience. I was having an experience within the kundalini as well. Oneness. Conduit. Souls Journey. Book.

The entire evening's experiences had rocked my inner world to its core. Had I made this up? I was rattled, in a good way, even though I could not comprehend any of it, not one single molecule of it. I had been initiated.

After my time in Bali, I settled into myself—my organic self—and reconstructed a new life. In this part of my journey,

I didn't seek a relationship, but I was open to what and who may come. I experienced the luxury of being enough! I more often chose to be responsive rather than reactive. It was easier to maintain a higher vibration and not spiral out of control. I enjoyed music more profoundly, not just singing along to songs in the car but participating in kirtan call-and-response singing as an act of devotion and really feeling it.

Wow, one of those journeys would have been enough but having them together was life altering. In my unconscious, unaware life prior to this, there was nothing magical, mystical, or expansive, I had experienced; I experienced more magic in *one* year than I had in the twenty-one years of being sober, collectively! I didn't know, what I didn't know and for me *everything* is about experience.

Let's talk about your experiences…

Have you had one (or many) epic spiritual experience(s)? If so, how has it shifted the way you now live your life? If not, as a suggestion, perhaps review the questions in the first chapter.

_____

_____

_____

_____

_____

_____

_____

❦ Does the thought of kundalini scare you or excite you? Why?

_____

_____

_____

_____

_____

_____

❦ What kind of magic do you want to create in your life?

_____

_____

_____

_____

_____

❦ Do you have any fears about expanding your level of consciousness with plant medicine?

_____

_____

_____

_____

_____

21

COLORADO BOUND!

I met Liv in the fall of 2019, and while Covid was at the forefront of everyone's life in 2020, I was steeped in my shadow-self. We worked from home, and living on nine acres made us feel only slightly different when we went into lockdown. I had been in my shadow for a few months and it progressively got worse as my excessive, destructive personality took over—literally took over. And it was big! It was a dark year for us both, both in our shadow in varying ways.

It was by far the darkest period of my life. Even though the earlier hopelessness was a rough period for me, it only impacted me. This was much worse, as my shadow self was rearing its ugly head and impacting Liv deeply; negatively affecting her fucked me up and was the reason for my spiral and self-sabotage. But as I would come to discover later, I was also in some deep medicine.

I didn't take care of myself emotionally, and that turned into not taking care of myself physically, mentally, spiritually, or energetically; it became just down-right painful. Everything I learned, everything I knew to be true for myself, appeared to go right out the window, and I plummeted—hard. This was the next layer in peeling back my onion.

It had gotten so bad that I planned to find a 30-day center, a holistic one in which I could do nothing but look further inward. After spending close to ten hours researching places, which was difficult because of the Covid lockdown or shutdown of businesses, I found a place in Glenwood Springs, Colorado, called 4Winds Farm, in August of 2020. And as the universe would see fit, it was the perfect place for me.

I was wound up like a fucking rubber band waiting to launch. I was so wound up energetically that it took me an entire week to land and get grounded. I had not seen this side of myself since I was 25 years old, when I had gotten sober. All my old behaviors were converging on me at once, and it was a total collapse in self-assessment and management, so it appeared. I was completely aware of my behaviors, but I was so in the middle of darkness that I could not see any light, anywhere.

I was actively participating in my beliefs, conditioning, and behaviors, some I knew I had and others, not so much. Over the many years in AA, I had also taken on many beliefs of Self that were not mine. These are not mentioned to blame others; rather, they showed me I can choose to believe my very own thoughts, thoughts I had created between my very own ears. The responsibility of my sovereignty lies only within me.

As time went on, I felt a lot calmer and started some intense work with a psychologist and a somatic therapist, who walked me through the trauma within my body. Losing my right breast was extremely traumatic, and while I had acknowledged this several times over the years, working in a somatic process got me back in touch with my body, allowing for the tears to roll down my face while embracing my very own self. It was incredibly healing for my spirit.

I felt as if I was starting to truly find myself again; I was true in my heart, letting go of what was not serving me any longer, feeling through my trauma.

Every single time I was met with the question by a thera-pist, "India, how do you feel about...?" My response was always, "I think..."

"That's nice," they would respond. "But I asked how you *feel*, not what you think."

"Aw!" I would respond. And we would have a good laugh.

I finally grasped the *feeling* part, and after a lot of process-ing, I realized I had remained in my head—not my heart—as a protection mechanism. I have always known how sensitive I am. I feel a lot. Sometimes I was berated or made fun of by another, and I didn't have a voice or confidence, so I just shut my heart down to protect myself. And I stayed there. I had pro-cessed so much in my short time at 4Winds, sharing the truth of my heart, where I was with Liv, my shadow self, my patterns, behaviors, and the trauma. I felt I was ready to return home.

*

I had been practicing the art of non-attachment for over a decade, which includes avoiding labels of good-bad, right-wrong, etc. These are identifiers of separation. My shadow wasn't wrong or bad or other; it simply was. It doesn't mean that my behavior didn't floor me or cause me emotional pain or pain to another, but I was keenly aware that we are each on our own path towards evolution and consciousness, and each step we take, each foot we plant, is necessary for that evolution.

If I label something negative, that insinuates that the experience that unfolded for me, or another person, shouldn't have been a part of the teaching for me or the other. Had I not had this experience of being deep in my shadow, I would not be working with others in the manner I currently do.

The Farm is where I found my *calling* and my *purpose*. While I was in my self-work, I would share my wisdom, strength, insight, and success of long-term sobriety. I shared within group my experience on starting my path to sovereignty, with women who were just beginning their journey of learning to live from the heart, not the head, who did not yet understand vibration, energy, frequency, or the journey of Self-discovery. It became very clear to me; this was my life's work. This is what all the teachings of my past were preparing me for; working to help others.

Since I had walked out of a recovery program after such a long time of being in the center of it and maintained my sobriety during major crises in my life, then started working with plant medicine ten years after, there was a lot of respect for what I had walked through, without self-medicating, when by all accounts, I needed to.

The interesting phenomenon about addiction is that society labels it as an outside-of-self issue. Society views the addiction, whatever it is, as *the* problem, when in fact the individual is lacking connection—connection to self or others, or the soul has been lying dormant and screaming for attention or lacks a purpose or meaning in one's life. The behavior results from any of these or all of them. Our culture does not see patterns of bad behavior such as anger, resentment, frustration, jealousy, righteousness, etc. as an addiction. But it most certainly is, and connection is not the same as socializing. Connection is being open and available to self and others with compassion and empathy. It's a state of BEing, tuning in to oneself to assess our emotional, spiritual, energetic, and physical needs.

In the chapter "Around the Bonfire," I elaborated on labels and the importance of not attaching ourselves to them. In Colorado, it appeared I was living in all the labels like "havoc," "damage," and "bad" behaviors – this is why I *don't use labels!* Every step of my journey was part of the process to get me where I am today. It doesn't mean I didn't *feel* remorse for my behavior toward Liv, I did, and I expressed that to her many times; however, I was also able to separate the spiritual teaching from the human behavior. Because every step in that process, from me being in my shadow to sending myself to Colorado, to working with the women there, 4 Winds brought me to exactly where I am today and why I do the work I do. I could not have come to this place had I not been in the human behavior. There were many beautiful outcomes that came out of my "shadow."

౿ Are you a thinker or a feeler? Most people are thinkers; we *think* our way through everything and start attaching labels to the feelings we're experiencing versus asking ourselves, "How does this situation make me feel?" Can you think of a situation in which you thought your way through the feelings? What if you sat for a moment, closed your eyes, dropped into yourself, and inquired within, "How did I feel in that moment?"

౿ I went to a trauma center and that might be looked at as "bad," but I needed it to discover my purpose at that place and time in my life. What have you experienced that was perceived by you and/or society as "bad," but was needed and lifechanging to the extent that it propelled you forward into thriving?

_____

_____

_____

_____

- Can you prioritize your *investment* in living aligned with your soul? After all, that's the reason you're here. Nothing is more important. What would it take for you to do so?

22

MY RITE OF PASSAGE

The new year had literally started off with a *Bang!* I loaded my car, said my sad goodbyes on the morning of New Year's Eve, 2020, and drove out of Glenwood Springs, headed west toward Utah. I stopped that night and rented a private space for the night because I planned to do a solo medicine journey in the beautiful red rocks of Moab, Utah. I sat in meditation for a short time, setting my intentions, and thinking about the new year that was now upon me. I ingested the psylocibin medicine around 7:00pm. It was a smaller dose than my normal ceremonial dose, and it would be my first-ever-solo-journey without a shaman.

As I laid in my bed, under the covers and on my back, I felt myself going deep, deep, deep into a place that I wasn't sure of – it didn't feel scary, rather I kept getting this feeling I was somewhere I should not have been – I didn't know where that was but rooted within the well of my Being, something did not feel right. I was rattled to my core. There was something I could feel, but I wasn't sure what it was.

I entered a realm I should not have been in and ended up in a very long night of medicine. It was not a journey of light and love like all my others had been over the years. No. This one took me down into an unfamiliar place. Throughout the evening, I just kept telling myself *I had the power to hold whatever it was I was experiencing.* It felt dark.

When I shared the news of this with my coach a few days later, she stated I had sent myself on a Rite of Passage. This Rite of Passage was the catalyst for me to fully understand that we are both the dark and the light. I had been avoiding the darkness in life - in my mind even though my behaviors reflected that of shadow. The combination of my human behaviors, and my soul's journey into the Underworld, was my initiation into my work.

I had the belief that I wanted to only be in the light and love; I wanted to disown the shadow, the darkness of my essence. It was then that I was able to embody all I needed in order to know that this was where I was led to do my work with others. If I can experience diving deep and arriving at the gates of Hell - spiritually, mentally, emotionally, ethereally - throughout my years of evolving, and have the ability to thrust myself out of all the darkness and back toward the surface, and into the light...

Then and only then, can I hold space for you.

23

FOLLOWING MY INTUITION

As I continue to sprout, grow, and have an excellent harvest, I no longer allow myself to spend my life-force on situations that don't hold a higher-energetic frequency, bring me joy, or challenge me at the highest level – which still happens often.

You are unique. Do you know your Divine Design? Do you delight in experiences that support your transformation? How well do you know yourself and what you are drawn to? I'm not talking about the wound of narcissism or an unhealthy self-focus that makes life smaller and more constrained and fucks up relationships. I'm talking about being a spiritual grown-up who is well served by making self-honoring choices that come from your deepest soulful desires.

Luxuriating in Divine love is an experience like no other. So how do you get there? Well, instead of you going through all the shit I went through, I can just teach you the lessons without you experiencing all deep pain and suffering. I will hand you the match to burn your house down, and I will be there with the fire extinguisher, just before you crackle, to put you out!

Take an inventory of what you've learned, what you've survived, what you've created, the skills, talents, insights you've gained along the way thus far. Can you relax into knowing all is well and always was and always will be? Is it possible that you can look back over your life and embrace and honor what you have managed to get yourself through, no matter how ungraceful it was? Can you see your strength and courage to walk through what was and be uncomfortable?

Meditation and prayer work. Quiet contemplation works. Time spent in nature works. And as I've suggested, time with the plants that have been given to us as spirit guides also works. As Michael Pollan puts it, "Everyday consciousness is not enough for us humans; we seek to vary, intensify, and sometimes to transcend it, and we have identified a whole collection of molecules in nature that allow us to do that."

Do you know why you are here? The answer is different for each of us. I know the answer for myself now. I had asked this question at ten, but just to myself, and I heard no answer and didn't have anyone to talk to. I abandoned the inquiry to fit in and follow what I thought I was supposed to do. I lived for decades, not knowing I could live my own sovereign life. I didn't even know what sovereignty meant. But once I understood how to live for myself, not through others or for others, but for myself and from devotion to Spirit and the direction provided by asking for guidance, I found myself in a place where I felt free of loneliness. I realized I needed to continually cultivate self-love and self-respect. A relationship with my Self was essential.

*

I am moved by how much we get out of being *in the world but not of it* for a time, shifting where we stand and stopping the clock for a while, so we can get quiet and connected and go deeper on our own and with others we love and trust. This is what humanity has always needed and what we are reawakening to discover. Stop. Withdraw for a time. Be quiet. Be aware. Do something unexpected. Follow your intuition.

When you're ready for what's next, ask for guidance, be silent, and listen. Let the past burn away. Blow the ashes into the wind. New ideas and inspirations will come. Take notes. Trust that what you receive in these more conscious states is important and is to be respected. When you're at a higher frequency, you access the courage to be true to your soul. Capture that inspiration in every way that moves you—in word, image, or a sacred object. This is rebirth. Make it real and concrete in every way you can think of to help lock in the progress.

Create a plan of action based on your deep commitment and include benchmarks and an organizational structure and a team that works. And then, and this is crucially important, get support for what it takes to achieve what you committed to do. Research shows that goals that are private are unlikely to be accomplished. The odds increase when you identify next steps and a timeframe. The odds increase again when you tell someone you love your dreams, and they are the type of person who believes in you and will have your back. These are the elements of success. To boost yourself into the stratosphere, add a skilled coach, one you resonate with, trust, and who can hold space for you. Put it all into physical form without getting stopped by your fearful shenanigans along the way.

Following through with integrity to completion is one of the most challenging aspects of transformation. Many people get stopped in the middle as soon as the fun of the vision process wears off. Pushing through is what separates those who fantasize but don't do, from those who make their dreams a reality.

*

I imagine the journey of life like this: Sometimes we're in the darkest fucking nights of the soul, absolutely convinced we're walking alone on the cold road, hiking up hill, in the dark, tired, and afraid. Alone and without support. We imagine we will always feel this sad, this depressed, this angry, this scared, this fucking lost and confused.

The dark night of the soul is a soul rebirth, a surrender to your *calling—to step into who you are and what life is asking of you now.*

In the shadowy places we live, we imagine every sort of threat hiding there and spin stories in our imagination, and energetically, it stays spinning there or lowers in frequency. Emotionally, it's taking form as resentment and moving into anger.

These ideas are painfully real until we shine light into the shadows and discover that fear is an illusion. The truth is that all there is, is love. Love that is not sentimental-greeting-card love, but the most powerful, fuel-for-everything-in-the-Universe kind of love.

Spirit is always present. Helpful people and influences are always there when we know how to recognize them, and we are *never alone.* Never. Ever. We are here on a journey to learn and evolve and remember who we are. We are each in a school with our own curriculum. We are here to transform ourselves and to make a difference in exactly the way we are uniquely designed. This I discovered in the light of Spirit.

The journey is hard on the rugged, uphill path of life. We shift. We pivot. We reset. We cultivate. We surrender. We offer support to fellow travelers. The opportunity of the darkest times is to reach even higher into the light; it is not possible to hold the ascension of these higher frequencies if we do not know of our shadow and work within it. This is the work we do together. The path to higher consciousness comes only from self-awareness, not our awareness of others; this is the conditioning most of us are in and live our entire lives in, then wonder why we're not fulfilled or happy.

I choose a big life rather than an ordinary one, so of course, the pressures and challenges that come with that are bigger. That's what comes with the territory. I choose to be responsible even when it does not feel good. I do better in some areas of my life than others. It's shifting and progress is being made. I need the body that's a fit for what I'm here to do with the stamina and strength to follow through. The snake is ready to shed her skin again. Time to dance it out, wriggle out of the old skin, and get it done. Because I want to.

& Take an inventory of what you've learned, what you've been through, and what you've created.

_____

_____

_____

_____

_____

_____

& Can you relax into knowing all is well and always was and always will be?

❧ Is it possible that you can look back over your life and embrace and honor what you have managed to get yourself through, no matter how ungraceful it was? Can you find compassion, grace, and self-love?

_____

_____

_____

_____

_____

_____

❧ Can you see your strength and courage to walk through what was uncomfortable? Can you honor that?

_____

_____

_____

_____

_____

_____

24

REBIRTH: RISE THEN FLY

The Dark Night of the Soul is just that, dark! It is a Soul rebirth, an experience so profound that many don't make it out the other side. Many people also don't know or understand what they're experiencing; it's a complete collapse of one's entire existence.

There was a day, years ago, when I knew I had to change my name; Cheryl was just not a vibrational match. Look at me. Do I look like a fucking Cheryl to you? There are many cultures where people change their names for a variety of reasons. For me, it marked a rite of passage, completing an initiation, shifting from one way of being to another—down to the name I would call myself and legally change, embodying all I have become. As I continued in deep mystical experiences where I was flooded with love and gratitude and a clear vision for the future, I was shown my blind spots—those places I had not completely grown into, the places where I would have to learn how to hold a higher frequency and I now do so with ease and grace.

I understood I was completely accountable to myself to monitor my responses and behaviors. The outcomes I created would be the measurement I would use to determine whether I was expanding or contracting. My new name would remind me to be vigilant about growth and would keep me on my toes. Cheryl might have been unaware. India is not.

The more I'm quiet, drop-in, let go, the more I choose to live in my heart, the more I come from a place of love and compassion for myself and others, the freer I become. The more I remain in my heart, the more I can hold nurturing space for myself and others. The way I remain in my heart is through self-reflection, meditation, plant medicine, processing and integration, and breathwork.

I've been living fully for some time now. My beautiful soul family reflects who I am.

Tonight is a celebration of my sixtieth orbit around the sun. Outside the floor-to-ceiling windows, the red rock landscape of Sedona is glowing. Inside this beautiful dining room, I'm seated at a large table with a beloved group of fifteen friends packed tightly around it. A couple of my scrawnier friends are even sharing one chair to fit at the overflowing table. This part of my tribe has gathered to celebrate another decade, another year, another day. My life overflows with sacredness and service. How did I become so truly abundant in every way? Early in life, I had been on a course to live a very destructive life had I not gotten sober. I was also on the path to exit life early, having caused substantial pain to those I love.

My current path is not one I sought; my higher self literally wanted me to succumb to the path I had been walking and then humbled me beyond measure, to take myself into the Dark Night of my own Soul. Yes, that is exactly what I did.

The magical, playful, and freeing life I live now looks like this: As we're seated at the table, we're in the home of friends whose playful marriage has generated a successful artistic career for him and a healing career and real estate entrepreneurship with a spark of genius for her. A wide circle of friends is drawn to this magical couple to bask in their warmth and generosity of spirit.

After I shared my gratitude and love for all those present and for all those who touch my life, we toast Larisa and our community, for the newly acquired land just outside Sedona on which we're building our retreat center, and her dream of community living. It's a special place on thirteen acres.

One friend, who has come from the south and lights up a room with her gregarious personality, is my rock, and a light worker. Next to her is a shamanic chiropractor and healer who works with imbalances at the level of spirit and soul. Another is a fourth-generation Philippine shaman who is drawn to grief work after decades of resisting it when her ancestors showed up, and she too went into her own Dark Night. She now sits proudly in who she is, embracing her exceptional healing gifts. Another beautiful soul is a light worker, and a crystal bowl vibrational alchemist, who channels the voices of ancient tribes and angelic realms.

Another friend, also a shaman who lives for spiritual service, has brought his animal companion, his snake, to dinner. After the meal, his snake wraps herself around the candelabra, her tail drawing back quickly when she accidentally gets too close to a burning candle as she ventures around the table to make new friends. The snake loves to ski. He explains how she nestles into his parka, wrapping herself around his shoulders and under his arms for warmth on the lift and then at the top of the slope slithers over his forehead with her tongue flicking to feel the wind in her face. I'm not kidding. These are the magical friends who make life a discovery of new play every day.

Each person at this table has a vision for how their life can continue to make a difference to others. All of us are committed to a higher ideal and to spiritual practice. These are the change-makers, the dreamers who are also *doers*.

My friend who's hosting tonight returned from a trip to Egypt with a headdress and necklace for me, reawakening my curiosity about why I've always been drawn there. One friend forgot I don't drink and gave me a bottle of wine—oops. The wine is enjoyed by other friends with the delicious food they've prepared for us with love. I have a special brew of tea as I celebrate the end of one chapter of life and the beginning of another.

Their birthday gifts are thoughtful, special, beautiful, and I am loved. So are they. My life could have looked so very different; I may not have made it to my thirties had I kept on the path I was on. I could have ended up in prison for alcohol-related issues; things could have looked so very different for me.

Now I am someone who guides and supports others on their journey of Self-Discovery through the shadow. You burn, you learn. You're empowered. You're Wise.

This process of birth, letting go, and rebirth are an ongoing cycle, and we evolve when we're tapped into our purpose and have the grit to continue. The world needs you at your full power and strength. Being stuck doesn't feel good. Fulfilling our soul's contract, mission and purpose can. The only way Out is In.

When I lived guided by my ego, I wouldn't have put myself on a spiritual path—but my higher Self did. When we stand in our sovereignty, our authentic selves, step into our gifts, embrace, and share these healing gifts, the world becomes a better place. Because of the process of rising again and again, I am here, alive, and well, laughing so hard I can hardly catch my breath. I'm softer now, a powerful force, but soft. I am stunned every time someone refers to me in this way. How can that be? While I can still be soft in my approach, I am direct, transparent, honest, and forthright. My responsibility is to empower others, by showing them one must travel the dark within, to come fully into consciousness. The shadow can be an unforgiving space if you do not understand or know how to process the lessons and teachings it is creating for you. I have the ability to guide you through the depths of that space, to bring you into awareness of the purpose and value of shadow – our very own teacher – and to not be afraid of it. I energetically and emotionally support you on all sides. I do not hold back the truth of what is being created around you, by you; it's my gift of being a seer. You can obtain harmony with your Shadow and your Light, growing and embracing all that you are and all that you can become. I only raise my voice to inspire something bigger and express something that's pointed toward transformation—mine and others.

I look around the table at the faces of these beautiful friends who are celebrating my 60th birthday. What a milestone after that decade. I couldn't have dreamed them up in my wildest fucking imagination. And yet it is clearly destined and impossible and unlikely and totally predictable that we would be here. Magic abound.

As we transform and look over our shoulder at where we've been, the bridge from our old life is burning, and that's a good thing. It's like the Vikings burning their boats, so they had no choice but to push forward and explore. We can't ever go back. The flame lights the way forward, and now we see more clearly where we're headed.

*

Thank you for the time you've spent with me in the pages of this book and the work you've done to take on many of these practices, thoughts, and suggestions. I hope you'll remember a story, think of a teaching when you need it, and smile when you see the humanity in us all. I'm honored you let me share a small part of my life's journey with you. Our paths have already crossed in these pages, so perhaps they will cross in another place and time as well - in a workshop, retreat, or course.

Until then, remember…

The only way *OUT* – is IN.

GRATITUDE—YOURS AND MINE

As you scan my acknowledgement of people who have contributed to my life, this book, and my work, I encourage you to take a few minutes to make your own list of those who have been there for you. Who guided, gifted, supported, and allowed you to support them, either briefly in passing, for the turning of a season, or a lifetime?

When we add up the contributions of others, it's fucking inspiring. And if you've lived a full and generous life, whatever that means for you, perhaps your name can show up on the lists of others who needed you the most. We all have a story; how do you want to tell the tale of yours?

THE HEALING TRIBE

I'm grateful for the many who went through the fire with me. It took an army of energy workers, light keepers, shamans, breath workers, soul retrieval practitioners, astrologers, numerologists, mediums, sound healers, alchemists, readers of akashic records, yoga teachers, breath work facilitators, masters of meditation, and doctors and nurses.

For supporting me through cancer I thank: M. Todd Williams, Janna Roncelli, Caryn Mark, Krisi Cleveland, Phyllis Nickelsen, Shauna Reynolds, Joan Fuller, Terrell Washington-Anansi, Stacy Young, Samantha West-Bradley, Kandice Brumley, Kohli Kick, Andy Qualls, Gilda's Club of Tennessee, Camp Blue Bird, and Murphy USA.

Janna, Caryn, Shauna, Phyllis, and Todd—who provided places for me to lay my head during chemo and many surgeries that followed. Living in one state while being treated in another is no easy feat. You provided nurturing, laughter, and love when I needed to receive it the most.

THE TRANSFORMATION TRIBE

Phyllis Nickelsen – You are one hell of a friend who listened while I was in a calamity, who showed up again and again for over 35 years. I cherish our friendship and all of who you are. I love you beyond measure.

Krisi Cleveland – You will always have a special place in my heart for your unconditional love and support. I am deeply grateful for you, for being such a compassionate human being.

Jeannie MacDonald – Thank you for embracing your gifts and sharing them with us. The soul's contractual agreement seed you planted was forever life changing. Thank You. I love and adore you.

The Soul of Yoga – In Encinitas, California, a home base for classes, learning workshops, live music, and teacher training lead by teachers who are extraordinary.

Chiara Stella – You are such a beautiful soul. Your perspective, knowledge, insight, love, compassion, nurturing ways, support, and sisterhood have had deep and profound impacts on my life. I love you to the moon and back—several times.

Larisa Stow-Norman – My beautiful friend and soul sister, I hold so much gratitude for your expansive compassion, open heart, and for guiding me so skillfully into a new way to live, a new way to Be. Thank you for lifting so many up through your music, teaching, and love. I would fly without wings or walk a thousand miles for you—in this lifetime or any other.

Liv Larssen – Thank you for enduring the darkest part of my shadow-self. I am so deeply grateful for you and all that you behold. So much love to you.

Brigette Schabdach – Founder of 4Winds Farm for the opportunity to hunker down and finish this book and meet up at the end of the day for endless belly laughs around the dinner table. I love you to pieces my sister Scorpio.

A SPECIAL THANK YOU

Angela Howard ~ for Inspiring me to write this book through your encouraging words and impactful ways. And I love you beyond measure. Thank you for all that we share – You're the Best!

Suzanne Stebila ~ for always being by my side as a mentor, friend, collaborator, comedian, sidekick, a soul sister, and a rock!!! Thank You, Thank You, Thank You!
I love you-twice around!

Morgan Kelce ~ What an amazing cycle of life we've been on together. Thank you for your contribution in the completion of this book, on so many levels, in so many ways, and for being just the perfect soul to do so. I am so grateful for you, and I love you to pieces.

DEDICATION

Aunt Charlotte ~ Passed away May 24, 2023 from the sudden on-set of cancer at 91 years young. You are forever my Hero!

To the Women in my family who have gone before me – The untethering sacrifices made. The strength, courage and will that you have displayed during the harshest of times is beyond measure. Thank You for your endless guidance from the other side.

And finally, I express gratitude for all the breakdowns and breakthroughs ahead because life is lived in cycles of burning and rising and things never really end…now do they!

FIRE BURNING CEREMONY

Grab a large candle, preferable one with three wicks and a box of toothpicks (any shape, size, color)
Now is the time to release, let go, and to surrender.

Sit comfortably. Close your eyes. Take a deep breathe into your heart space and release. Drop into yourself. Pick up one toothpick and hold it in your hand, now bring your hand to your heart. Think about *letting go* of what this toothpick represents—any hurt, what you might have guilt about, a list you made, painful thoughts you bravely wrote, hardships you boldly went through, or maybe hardships you partook in. This is for *you*, so whatever you want to let go of, think of that.

Take a deep breath into your heart space, then out. Take a second breath in, and on your breath out, hold your hand with the toothpick up to your mouth and blow out all that which you are giving away, that which does not serve you, onto the toothpick. Take a moment and *take it in*—not relive, not revisit—just take it in and notice how it makes you feel. Whatever arises, just let it be, without judgment. Place the toothpick into the wax in the middle of candle, near the wick. Take another deep breath in and out. When you are ready, light this first toothpick with a match (or lighter, whatever you have) and watch it completely burn.

Pick up another (second) toothpick and hold it to your heart. Think of what you want to *receive* from this thing you let go of with the first toothpick. It could be receiving love, freedom, heart-centeredness, compassion, being judgment free, forgiveness, acceptance, or whatever comes to your mind that you want to bring into your heart, your BEing. Take a breath in and out. Take a second breath in, keeping in mind what you are receiving, and on your breath out, blow onto the toothpick in your hand, as though you're breathing what you're gaining from this toothpick to life. Take another moment to *take this all in*, without judgment. Place the toothpick into the wax in the middle of candle, near the other toothpick and wick. Take another deep breath in and out. When you are ready, light this second toothpick and watch it completely burn.

Pick up the last, the third, toothpick and hold it to your heart. Think of who or what you want to *thank, pray for, or have gratitude towards*. Usually the person who irks you the most or maybe even the person that was part of the questions you answered are the best ones to pray for, to thank, and to have gratitude towards. *What!? Yuck!* I know. But this is how you stay in heart. Take a breath in and out. Take a second breath in, keeping in mind this person, place, or thing and breathe that out onto the toothpick you're holding. *Take this all in*, without judgment. Place the toothpick into the wax in the middle of candle, near the other two toothpicks and wick. Take another deep breath in and out. When you are ready, light this third toothpick and watch it completely burn.

When the third toothpick has gone out, sit and have gratitude for all that it represents. Watch it dance while burning – taking different shapes and color – it can be beautiful and destructive (like lightness and darkness!) Did some of your toothpicks burn brighter, rougher, or longer than others? Did some seem empowering and validating in how they burned? Did some seem anticlimactic? It all burned exactly as it should.

Light the candle you used and allow it to burn away the burnt ends of the toothpicks or for the ends to fall into the wet, melted wax. You can walk away from now, hopefully feeling lighter, brighter, and a little more renewed and empowered. (Remember to blow out the candle!)

You can use this ritual for anything. You can do it at the end of every day and think of circumstances that happened throughout the day. Give it to the Fire - It's a great practice.

Enjoy!

Do you know the story of Persephone?
It's a beautiful metaphor for the Shadow.

Persephone is the daughter of the Greek God, Zeus, and Demeter, the Goddess of Harvest and Fertility. Persephone was so beautiful and captivating that every man and God took notice, but Demeter, who was overprotective of her only daughter, would not allow any man, or God, to come near her. One day, Hades came across Persephone and was taken aback by her beauty, grace, and aliveness. Hades asked her mother, Demeter, if he could marry her, to which she responded that her daughter would never marry Hades, who only had dead people for company; the underworld is far from deserving to be bestowed with Persephone's presence. Hades was heartbroken and mad, and he decided he would take Persephone either way.

One day, while Persephone was outside on her own, Hades created a crack in the Earth and came up, grabbed her, and took her down to the Underworld in his chariot. No one knew what happened to Persephone (except Zeus and the God Helios, the Sun, but they kept their mouths shut so as not to anger the God of the Underworld). Once Demeter found out Hades was Persephone's captor, she was beyond approach, distraught, grief stricken and depressed. To punish the Gods, she refused to fulfill her Goddess duties of Harvest and Fertility, so the Earth went into total decline. The crops died, animals died, water dried up, everything became dark, grey, and dead. Something needed to be done, and in the end, it was agreed that Persephone would be Hades's wife and would stay in the Underworld for half of the year, and for the other half, she would come home to Olympus and be with her mother, Demeter.

For six months, Persephone goes into the dark, the shadow, the death, and when her time is done there, for she does not stay in the dark for too long, she births to the Earth again, the light. It is said when she is in the Underworld, we have Fall and Winter, and when she comes up to Earth, like being reborn, we have Spring and Summer. Death and Life, Death and Rebirth, Dark and Light, Shadow to anew and Glowing.

REFERENCES

Pollan, Michael, (pg. 32) *This is Your Mind on Plants,* First Edition, Penguin Press, July 6, 2021.

Whatismypiritanimal.com, Sea Urchin Medicine, Building Beautiful Souls, Inc. 2023, https://whatismyspiritanimal.com/spirit-totem-power-animal-meanings/fish/sea-urchin-symbolism-meaning/

The Mankind Initiative, (2023) "Statistics on Male Victims of Domestic Violence," The Mankind Initiative, Helping Men Escape Domestic Abuse, https://www.mankind.org.uk/statistics/statistics-on-male-victims-of-domestic-abuse/

Greeka, (2004) "Persephone, Queen of the Underworld," Greeka, Greece-Myths, https://www.greeka.com/greece-myths/persephone/

ABOUT THE AUTHOR

 India Zoe Prema has been to hell and back with addiction, alcoholism, cancer, financial losses, medical crises, and close relationships that crashed and burned. She knows the grip of anger, isolation, illness, loneliness, depression, and uncertainty.

That's the value of what she teaches in her work and how she guides individuals and families to transcend the darkest nights of the soul. India has found that it's worth it to walk through fire to transmute trauma, cultivate self-awareness, find self-love and to experience magic beyond the ordinary.

India wrote this book from her home in the deep canyons and red-rock buttes of Sedona, Arizona. However, she's always ready to travel when inspired to do so because she's committed to letting life led her to where she can grow and where she's needed by those she serves.